Coaching For The Zone

A Practitioner's Guide to Coaching for Business and Sport

by Ted Garratt

BENNION KEARNY

Published in 2014 by Bennion Kearny Limited.

Copyright © Bennion Kearny Ltd 2014

ISBN: 978-1-909125-40-7

Published by Bennion Kearny Limited
6 Woodside
Churnet View Road
Oakamoor
ST10 3AE

www.BennionKearny.com

To Catherine for making it all worthwhile and Archie for
his constant support, motivation, positivity and presence – plus his
willingness to let me take him for a walk every time I got stuck.

Acknowledgements

One of the odd things about writing a book is that for an experience that is so individual it requires a lot of input, insight, and support from others. This book is no exception.

Along the way many people have contributed, some by their support, some by their example, some by just being themselves. Among many people who fit these categories I would particularly like to thank: Bob Wheeler, Reg Adair, Mick Weir, Geoff Haddon, John Coe, Bob Banister, Miles Peacock, Tim Boon, James Whitaker, Paul Clarke, Kev Vernon, Dave Kitching, Tony Moore, John Porter, Aidan Mernin, Alison Schreiber, Paul & Helen Craven, Chris & Alison Howgate, Elaine & Martin Pickering, Kate Salmon and Ian Jay, John & Shirley Bevington, Ian & Gerry Perkins, Jane & Bill Ballard-Warren, Ross Clarke, Will Jefferson, Jeremy & Louise Hill, Andy & Deidre Wiggin. Finally to all the coaches, support staff, and players at Leicestershire CCC.

This journey would not have been possible, or half the fun it has been, without these people and many others who helped along the way.

About the Author

Ted Garratt's career began in Human Resources Management in the manufacturing sector, where his interest in people development grew and quickly became a passion. He has worked all over the world during his diverse career, providing specialist coaching and mentoring for a vast number of organisations including Dyson, Aggregate Industries, Alstom Power, Akzo Nobel, International Paint, Uniq Foods, Leicester Tigers and England Rugby.

A significant interest in Ted's life is writing and he is the author of two books 'The Effective Delivery of Training Using NLP' and 'Sporting Excellence', which have both been published in a number of languages. Ted has an MA in Coaching and Mentoring, where his dissertation was 'What is the Zone, can it be coached, and if so how?' Ted uses this approach in his daily work in both business and sport.

Table of Contents

Introduction

What is Coaching?

Coaching is all about improving performance. Coaching is not remedial.

In sport, improvement can often be quite obvious and tangible (times run, distances thrown, points scored). But, outside sport, there may be dozens of other measures that people will be working to improve on. Some of these will be hard edged measures; e.g. in an organisation they may be based on performance appraisals, return on investment, cost-benefit analyses, 360° feedback, more effective recruitment, better retention of people, greater productivity, results of projects. For individuals outside organisations they may include: better health, greater fitness, better relationships, more success either at work or in carrying out a hobby. The measures for these and the evidence for being in the Zone will be agreed between the coach and the coachee.

What is the Zone?

The Zone is a mental performance state, where you don't have to think about what you are doing. It is characterised by total absorption in an activity, where skills execute totally naturally.

The Zone has been described in a number of ways:

- effortless ease
- accomplished mastery
- going with the flow

Coaching For The Zone

Interestingly, people get so absorbed in the moment, that they often do not realise they are in the Zone, at the time. It is based upon being on automatic pilot and going 'beyond' whatever one thought possible previously.

The Zone is relevant for a number of reasons, one of which is the added dimension it gives to people's lives. Even though they may not use the word 'Zone', people often describe transcendent, life changing, or life affirming experiences that relate to the Zone.

- 'It just felt right'
- 'I was on automatic pilot'
- 'I could do no wrong'
- 'It just fell into place'

From my experience, as a practitioner, the Zone is a universal state, and can apply across all individuals and all contexts.

Why would someone want to enter the Zone?

The Zone is a transformational process that enables people to perform to a higher ability and standard. As mentioned above, the best known application is within sport; athletes talk about being 'in the Zone' at the point of either winning or achieving results that they have never achieved before.

Some examples are Will Jefferson, the former Leicestershire cricketer when playing the Super Over that won the 2011 T20 Final at Edgbaston, Jonny Wilkinson dropping the goal that won the 2003 Rugby World Cup, Didier Drogba scoring the penalty that won the 2012 Champions League for Chelsea, Andy Murray winning Wimbledon in 2013. Therefore people want to enter the Zone so that they can achieve a particular result, or performance, or 'go beyond themselves.'

What about people who are not sportsmen and sportswomen? What about the account manager or the widget company salesman?

One of the great things about the Zone is that it is a life process, in that you can be anything – businesswoman, doctor, gardener, pianist – anybody in any walk of life can benefit from learning to enter the Zone state.

Some people will argue that because some aspects of the Zone are elusive, and difficult to pin down (such as effortless ease or automatic pilot) it is not possible to coach it. In my experience, this is not the case as everyone I have worked with has experienced the Zone but often without realising it, or in a different context or situation to the one they are now trying to work on. The power of this is that if they have had the experience, whatever the context, the door is open to achieving it again.

People cannot discover new oceans unless they have the courage to leave the shore.

Andre Gide

But, on a practical level, what will the Zone actually do for people?

The Zone will help take performance beyond what has been achieved before. For example, if giving a presentation is required, but the presenter is terribly nervous, entering the Zone state means that they will be able to perform more effectively.

In turn, the Zone can help people become more creative, develop better work relationships, improve their performance, increase skills or confidence.

Example: The Zone in Action

A teacher (a friend of mine) was having difficulties with her class and with one individual in particular who was the ring leader for the whole class. This individual was rude, aggressive and confrontational and my friend was at her wits' end as to how to deal with him.

Finally she achieved a breakthrough with the boy not by trying to force or dominate him but by using humour. Humour that did not just laugh with him, or at him, but which operated in a purposeful direction.

The *significance* of this is that it was done on the spur of the moment not preordained. When discussing this afterwards she said that *had* she pre-thought her actions, she would *not have* felt she had the skill or the confidence to do as she did. Therefore she would not have attempted it.

The teacher said she had heard of the Zone, without understanding what it was, but when she described how she *felt* while achieving this breakthrough in class, she was describing the Zone beautifully. She responded automatically without conscious thought, trusting her intuition, prepared to trust her skills and instincts in order to respond effectively to the situation.

Example: The Zone Outside Sport

I was working with a professional cricketer (he was struggling for performance at the time of our sessions) who had experienced being in the Zone many times within his sport.

As part of the coaching process, I asked whether he had experienced the Zone outside his sport. "No," he replied. "The Zone is only experienced within cricket."

Then he paused, and began to recount an occasion when he was best man at a wedding and had to stand up and give a speech to 400 people. Something that, frankly, made him extremely nervous. Five minutes into the speech, he was totally in-synch with the event. He could look around, see faces, was aware of the power of his voice. He was, in fact, in the Zone.

The two examples above, illustrate how the Zone can operate without an individual knowing it, or - when someone is trained in the Zone - in other/different parts of their lives.

Example: The Zone in Business

I was coach to a businessman who had a total fear of presentations. Although a very successful senior manager he avoided giving presentations to the point where it became obvious and visible to other people.

Through coaching it became apparent that he was more worried about things going wrong than positive about the benefits of getting it right. Through a combination of techniques covered in this book, anchoring, visualisation, belief changes, his mindset was changed from getting it right for *himself* to getting it right for his *audience*. He learned how to utilise the Zone.

This change was huge for him as it enabled him to liberate himself and push and extend his comfort zones way beyond anything he had ever imagined.

One other added benefit to this was that he realised that this change of attention was powerful in all aspects of his everyday life, both at home and at work. Although he had always considered himself a good people manager this ability to pay more attention, on a deeper level, to other people reaped dividends outside the narrow field of giving presentations.

So, how easy is it (for a coachee) to learn the Zone?

People often look for a quick fix to their problems, but learning the Zone requires repetition and it requires practice. In a nutshell, it requires a *commitment*.

Personal excellence is only possible if you have a dream and plan and if you persist in the face of all obstacles.

Unknown

Coaching For The Zone

This book is about coaching the Zone; does that mean enabling coachees to enter the Zone more easily?

Yes, but not just more easily - more regularly too. Often, people report that they believe they entered the Zone spontaneously during a presentation or meeting or activity. The aim of this book is to enable coaches to train coachees to enter the Zone on demand.

How easy is it to coach for the Zone?

From the coach's perspective? It is incredibly easy, with the right preparation. But preparation is key!

How many sessions are normally required for a coaching for the Zone programme?

Hah! How long is a piece of string? Some people will get it very quickly. One of the reasons for this is that many people (without necessarily realising it) will have had experience of the Zone previously, and this will come out during discussions.

Normally, I find anything from three to nine sessions is applicable.

Frequency is a related issue to the number of sessions. In sport, for example, the coach might have regular contact with the coachee (weekly maybe) whilst in the business environment the frequency might be monthly or six-weekly. High frequency will shorten the process though not necessarily the number of sessions.

Often I find that coachees (between the first and second, or second and third session) will come back and say "I had this experience in this meeting / at this presentation / with this client – and I think that was the Zone because…" This can then affect the number of sessions, and their content.

Do coachees need the Zone to solve particular problems, or do they need the Zone to expand their abilities?

It is a bit of both. A lot will depend on the job and the context. Some people will be extremely specific and it is about improving their job performance - in the here and now - in a measured way. They will want to demonstrate to themselves, and maybe their managers, the success that has been achieved.

Other people will find the Zone slightly more 'peripheral'. These folks are looking to gain different skills and different attitudes, and a trust in the process will enable them to apply the Zone when required.

Who This Book Is For

The main audience for this book is obviously coaches; irrespective of the context in which their coaching takes place.

However, other people who could benefit from the book and, in particular, the activities include:

- Individuals from any sector or background who wish to improve their performance
- Managers who wish to improve their abilities in managing people
- Teams who wish to expand their skills and improve their performance
- Anyone interested in improving their own self-development
- People with a special interest in the field of improving human performance
- Anyone interested in getting involved in the field of coaching

How To Use This Book

The purpose of this book is to help managers, coaches, coachees and potential coaches to achieve new levels of performance by accessing the Zone on a more consistent basis. Therefore, making best use of the book will depend to large extent on the interests of the reader.

One way to use the book would be to go straight to the activities parts of each section. However, conducting the activities without understanding the context or being able to respond to the coachee's real requirements can be inappropriate and even potentially damaging.

Coaching For The Zone

The Coaching Sessions With Alan

The first part of this book centres around a coaching program with 'Alan'. The sessions with Alan provide a framework for the rest of the book in that most of the sessions include a description of a situation that Alan is facing, how the situation is dealt with, a sample dialogue between Alan and the coach, a case study from sport, and one or more activities to use to improve the coaches skills.

The Purpose of The Key Skills Section

One of the anomalies of the Zone is that although it can be difficult to describe it can be achieved on a regular basis by the coach using a wide range of key skills.

What is even more powerful and helpful is that these key skills are not magical or mysterious but are actually the same skills that people use all the time in their everyday lives. It's in the *application* of these skills that the skill of the coach comes into play – providing 'the difference that makes the difference'.

So the purpose of the key skills section is to offer a set of skills that the coach can use with their coachees, and also use to develop their own effectiveness. Skills such as questioning, giving and receiving feedback, using intuition, dealing with self-limiting beliefs, and more, are covered in a similar way to the sessions with Alan. Let's begin!

Session 1

> **"** *The will to succeed is important, but what is more important is the will to prepare* **"**
>
> **Bobby Knight**

As a coach, I am about to start a 'coaching for the Zone programme' with a new coachee (Alan). What do I need to do first?

As ever, the first thing is to be thoroughly and totally prepared. People often look at preparation as hard work; does it really need to be done? Yes. It requires preparation in the same way as preparing for a presentation, appraisal, meeting, sporting event, hobby, or even a fun night out.

The coach should prepare to get the coaching session right for the coachee, not themselves. If they don't do this they run the risk of running a prescriptive, unhelpful session that will not help the coachee unblock and move forward. Inevitably this will not help the coachee (in this case Alan) improve their ability to get into the Zone on a more regular basis.

What does the coach need to know?

In a business context (or a sporting one for that matter), the coach needs to have an insight into the organisation they are working for (corporate culture, the business climate, any processes they use which would include appraisals and 360° feedback, plus other ways of defining performance and/or giving feedback to individuals and teams). However, I would suggest the coach avoids preparing to work with a coachee under a 'pre-set agenda', particularly one that is not owned by the coachee.

Coaching For The Zone

In order to flesh out the above, it may be useful for the coach to understand and/or discuss the following:

- The coachee's relevant job description
- The results of any 360° feedback, psychometric tests, or appraisals
- Feedback received via the organisation's performance management process
- Any competency frameworks the organisation may use – including key ones for the coachee's role
- Training courses/programmes previously attended, plus comments on their effectiveness
- If available, why Alan is interested in the Zone and what experiences he has of the Zone

All of these need to be acted on (preferably) as part of the preparation phase so that the first session goes as well as possible.

How the preparation is carried out will inevitably impact on the effectiveness of the actual coaching process. This may not be immediately apparent but it's rather like the iceberg, the preparation is the part of the iceberg that is hidden beneath the water!

A personal anecdote

Due to having seen a number of people before one particular client, I didn't take the time to physically, or mentally, prepare for a session and suddenly found myself in a situation which was rapidly going off the rails.

As soon as I realised this, rather than blunder on and hope (or pretend) that things would be okay, I openly told the coachee what I had noticed, checked with him that my perception was accurate, apologised for not being ready, and explained what I would normally do to prepare properly.

He was intrigued a) by the apology b) by the fact that there was a preparation process I normally followed. He explained that he had not realised this and assumed that I just turned up and we 'had a chat'. This led to him telling me he had an important meeting coming up and, while he had prepared the content, he hadn't considered preparing mentally.

Our first session then became a session around helping him prepare for this meeting and we agreed to postpone any discussion on further objectives regarding the Zone until the second session and after the meeting, so that he could decide on how effective the coaching and the mental preparation for the meeting had been.

What about suitable preparation for the coach himself / herself?

The coach needs to undertake mental preparation before any session. It is about being clear about your own skills, your own style, and what you are looking to achieve.

Some useful self-reflection questions for the coach at this stage can include:

1. What personal skills and tactics do I want to focus on at the coaching session?
2. What will be the evidence/measures of my success?
3. What specific actions do I need to take to practice the skills or tactics?
4. What beliefs do I have regarding my ability to improve my skills?
5. How do I think my experiences of coaching for the Zone need to be updated/reviewed before I start my next session ?

Coaching For The Zone

The first session is about to begin. Do you have any recommendations for environment, how to dress, how to position furniture? What is best practice to enable the session to succeed?

There are a number of very positive ways to help a session succeed. The environment should have no interruptions; distraction should be kept to a minimum. The environment should not be antiseptic, the coachee needs to feel comfortable and not feel they are being 'set up'. Having said that the room/environment needs to feel natural and relaxed. I often use hotel lobbies as these have a 'buzz' about them without being intrusive; some people think this is an odd choice because of the noise factor, however I have found it to be more relaxing for the coachee as it is common to be more relaxed and private in an open environment. Often, of course, the client (e.g. an employer) will provide a meeting room for the sessions and this is obviously fine.

Is there a recommended length of time for the first session?

Books offer a wide range of answers to this question. From my experience, 90 minutes seems about right. In fact, most sessions should be of this length because - oddly enough - there is a danger of having too *much* time. This can result in using time that is not required and going 'round the houses' which results in confusion, lack of clarity, and lack of commitment at the end of the session. Knowing when to stop is a key skill for getting the coachee into the Zone.

Should there be a break in this 90 minute session?

Yes, allow for comfort breaks and coffee breaks, even a stroll around.

The session starts. What's first?

Greet the coachee, preferably by name (Alan). Make them comfortable within the room. Start the process.

As with all coaching, the key thing is to avoid launching into explaining all about yourself and what the coaching is designed to do. Flag up that you are willing to do this, if desired, but (particularly for the first session) it is important for Alan to explain all about his skills, background, and experiences and, specifically, what he wants to get out of the coaching process. And - if he is familiar with the Zone – where the Zone fits in.

The opening to the session should include:

- A personal introduction; plus what you do, and how you do it - but be concise. There will be lots of opportunities and better times to get into this.
- Check what Alan knows about coaching in general and any quick insights he has into the Zone
- Clarify and deal with any issues on Alan's attitude to coaching
- Establish what the coachee's first thoughts are regarding what they want to get from the coaching process. (Remember, this should not be cast in stone, it will almost certainly change during the process)
- Establish protocols for working together including meeting dates or times, contact between sessions, confidentiality
- Agree initial action steps.

As the coaching process unfurls, should I use personal examples or should I leave this alone (basically depersonalizing myself from the process)?

It is important that there is a connection, a rapport, with Alan. However, the way not to achieve that is by telling personal stories and anecdotes too soon. The criteria is that they need to be relevant to the situation - and Alan - not just your favourite stories!

Are there any secrets for establishing rapport?

Rapport is one of the major skills for any coaching programme. It is a combination of interest in the other person, listening, and (perhaps oddly) asking the right questions. It is about stimulating, stretching and challenging Alan in a purposeful way so that he goes away engaged with the process and the coach, and is willing to take on challenges. If this is not attained, the Zone can still be achieved for Alan but it may make it harder.

[Rapport is covered in depth in the *Key Skills* section of this book].

Coaching For The Zone

When I sit down with Alan for the first session, is it important we map out what we are looking to accomplish overall?

Yes (as mentioned above), but not too soon. In turn – and down the line – in virtually all of my coaching for the Zone experiences, aims and targets have changed along the way. Often, by the third or fourth session, a coachee will come in and say that although the first couple of sessions were valid, now that they have been through the process – they have a clearer and more concrete idea of what they want to accomplish.

So, coaching needs a shape and needs a structure but being too programme-driven (too soon) will normally damage the process. The following questions – from the coachee's perspective - can be used to help determine structure.

1. What is my (e.g. Alan's) desired outcome from the session(s)?
2. What does this outcome say about me as a person, my beliefs, strengths, weaknesses?
3. How will I know that I have achieved my goals from the coaching session?
4. What thoughts do I have regarding any issues. skills or situations I want to work on? Why have I chosen these? Should I keep a written list of my outcomes and progress? If so, should this list be updated on a regular basis?
5. How will I reward myself when my outcome for the session has been achieved?
6. What do I already know about the Zone? What previous experiences have I had of the Zone (or something similar)? Why am I interested in the Zone? How do I want to use it?

During the Session, I have established rapport with Alan, I have identified some areas where Alan wants to take himself (in relation to the Zone) – how do we draw this first session to close?

Start by summarizing the key points of the session. Let Alan do this (as there is a real danger, otherwise, that the coach launches into their view of the session which (because of the newness of the relationship) Alan may acquiesce to and accept. Before the next session (planned and agreed at that point) the coach and Alan need to agree what specific actions Alan (and the coach as appropriate) is to undertake between sessions. [An example follows this session]

*[Between Sessions, the Coach and Alan have agreed
that Alan will complete the following Task]*

Zone Reflection Diary

What will this task accomplish?

It will provide a framework for the coachee, Alan, to reflect on his development
to identify whether the Zone is being entered (or what approximates to the Zone)
during regular day-to-day actions. The contents of the reflections should be based
on actions Alan has carried out, which may be day-to-day events or a specific
task (e.g. making more impact at a meeting, or thinking about and reviewing
actions and their impact on himself and other people).

When should the coach use it?

Daily

How long should it take?

10 minutes

Instructions for the Coachee

Fill in the table thinking about your daily experiences with particular regard to
any Zone-like experiences. Take time to reflect fully…

Day	Time	Date	Skill	Duration	Comments	Quality (1-10)
Monday						
Tuesday						
Wednesday						
Thursday						
Friday						
Saturday						
Sunday						

Session 1 – Sample Dialogue

This sample dialogue takes place as part of the conversation into Alan's knowledge/experiences of the Zone.

Coach: So Alan what do you know about the Zone?

Alan: Well I have heard it mentioned in interviews with sports people.

Coach: What sense do you get of 'what the Zone is'?

Alan: It seems to be a state where people can do tasks well, without really trying.

Coach: That's a good description. Do you have any personal examples?

Alan: That's a good question. I must admit I always thought the Zone was only about sport but in talking to family, friends and people at work - a number of them describe experiences which sound like the Zone.

Coach: So what about you?

Alan: I'm not sure but there was a time when I was able to deliver on a project under enormous pressure and at really short notice.

Coach: Tell me about it.

[Alan goes into detail regarding the project and his experiences when carrying it out.]

Coach: There is some really powerful stuff in there; before we go into it in more detail, do you have any similar experiences from outside work?

Alan: Hmmm, how about the time I was watching a movie on TV and got totally involved and absorbed by it? Could that count?

Coach: Yes, absolutely right, that could be an example. Tell me more about it.

Alan: The main thing I remember is being so involved I totally lost track of time.

Coach: Anything else?

Alan: Well I've never been the greatest   at following plots and understanding what is going on, but this time I got it all.

Coach: Why do you think that was?

Alan: I'm not sure this makes sense but I think it was partly because I wasn't trying too hard and just went with the flow.

Coach: That could well be. Let's go into more detail regarding your experiences.

[A further 10 minutes is spent discussing Alan's experiences inside and outside work, why he is interested in the Zone, and how he wants to use this as the session continues.]

Session 1 – Case Study – Sport

This case study is about a professional golfer who was managing to maintain a career and earn a reasonable living without actually making any progress or getting better. On one level he was comfortable with this but on another level he was frustrated and felt that other people were overtaking him. He came to me because I had worked with someone he knew in another sport, and that client thought I may be able to help. For context, the golfer had heard about the Zone without fully understanding it, and was willing to find out more.

In Session One we explored (as we would do in a business, teaching, parental or other environment) the golfer's background, how he had got into the sport, where he 'was' currently, and what he wanted to achieve. Taking this history took him by surprise but I explained that it was normal practice and was a vital step in the process. As part of the background conversation, we discussed his mental approach and he realised that he did have experiences of the Zone but fleetingly and with long gaps in-between.

The key points that emerged were that he had always lacked confidence in his abilities. In fact, in every situation he found himself in (e.g. home, school and even with his friends) he lacked confidence. He had actually started to play golf because of social pressure, not because he was good at it and wanted to play. This emerged as part of the conversation and he said that he had never told anyone this before, partly because he had never fully realised it.

This discovery shook him up quite a lot and actually made him more nervous. He was not sure whether he liked what he had discovered and not sure whether he wanted to start/continue with the process. However, the brief moments when he had been in the Zone were the high points of his *life* (not just his golf) and this created the spur that encouraged him to make the decision to start on the process, commit to it, and see what came out of it.

At this point I worked on creating rapport by asking him a number of questions to help him think through not just how this situation had developed - but more about how he had dealt with it, and what he had achieved both in golf and in the rest of his life. The key to this was to allow him to discover things for himself, rather than point them out to him (i.e. to allow him to own his successes and build on his previous experiences of the Zone).

We planned our second session for four weeks after session 1. The actions he committed to, between sessions, included – making a list of his achievements in all aspects of his life, making a list of his specific achievements in golf, and looking for the patterns and themes that had emerged (along with the skills and experiences) from the Zone he had experienced.

Session 2

Session two is about to begin. Seated with Alan, what should we do first?

The first thing I would normally do is get Alan to give me a five or ten minute update on their activity since the last session. That could be for the last week, last month, whatever. This feedback would not necessarily be about the coaching alone – it is very important that Alan gets the opportunity to talk through what has happened in any realm he wishes to discuss. Later, down the line, some of that information will almost certainly come around again, and be useful.

Okay, we are 10 minutes in. Alan has recounted his last few weeks. Is this the point to look at the task you set at the end of Session 1?

Yes. Absolutely right. At the end of Session 1, Alan was tasked to go away and complete a Review Diary to which he agreed, and committed to. This is now the opportunity to review how the process went.

Coaching For The Zone

Alan has come back with a great piece of work that recalled previous experiences when he thought he might be in the Zone. What do we do with this information?

The key at this point is to try and get more specific information, and move beyond the general point of being in the Zone.

- What was the context?
- What actually happened?
- In what sequence?
- What preparation, if any, went into being in the Zone?
- At what point did Alan become aware of being in the Zone?
- How did it feel?
- How did it impact on performance?
- What did Alan feel he could take from that experience that he could utilise to get into the Zone in the future?

So, we are recognizing, and teasing out, the elements that made up Alan's experience?

Yes. Equally, a coachee such as Alan might say, "I couldn't think of any Zone experiences from my past," and this is where going back to the first 10 minutes of the session (the general update) can often be the point where Alan (or the coach) realises that Alan *has* had an experience of being in the Zone. He has just not realised it. This is just as powerful (sometimes more so) than Alan coming back with two or three specific examples.

Although it seems not a lot has happened in this session, we have ended up with a few – quite detailed – examples of when Alan was in the Zone. Where do we take the session next?

The first part of the session was trying – without being prescriptive – to find out how Alan recognised he was in the Zone and what particular skills (intuition, curiosity, pushing beyond a comfort Zone, overcoming a limiting belief) Alan felt were part of it.

Having done that, and to whatever extent one can, the next step is to look forwards and begin looking at what Alan has coming up. In sport, it might be a specific performance. In business, it might be a presentation. Alan must start to think, based on his previous and current experiences, what specific steps can be taken (enabled by the coach) to get into the Zone next time.

It turns out that Alan has a massive business presentation in one month's time. Alan feels that his career, rightly or wrongly, hinges on this presentation. Is this a good event – or is it too big at this stage – to aim for with the Zone?

Inevitably, the answer is: 'it depends'. My personal style and philosophy is: *if it's real and it's live – go for it.*

So, no little steps to the big one?

If this is how the situation unfolded, I would personally feel very uncomfortable (and that I was not helping Alan) if I deferred him tackling the big presentation. I would use the presentation as an opportunity to embed the content we were discussing – and get Alan to practise getting into the Zone for the presentation. When Alan subsequently completes it, in a month's time, it gives us a meaningful event to review.

My experience is that most coachees, at this point in the process, will not expect things to be perfect or work every time. If Alan, for example, felt better having done the presentation (than it would if he did not try to utilise the Zone) then we have a much better proving point than deferring for six months.

Coaching For The Zone

Session two feels like it is coming to a close. We have identified an event in the future where Alan needs, and wants, to excel. Is this a good point to task Alan for out-of-session work for that experience?

Absolutely. As seen at the end of session one, and between all sessions, there will always be some form of tasking. On some occasions, it might involve reading a book or article but – more often than not – it will be 'go do' rather than 'go think about'. In sport it can be easy – there is always practice, there is always training.

The classic part of this is to ensure that people do not wait until just before the moment of performance. Coachees need, along the way, to be practising their skills.

*[Between Sessions, the Coach and Alan have agreed
that Alan will complete the following Task]*

Visualization

What will this task accomplish?

It will help the coachee practice and develop the correct techniques needed to carry out a task.

When should the coachee use it?

The coachee should do it daily for a week, then whenever required.

How long should it take?

Approximately 10 minutes, dependent on the task.

Instructions for the Coachee

Choose a particular skill or ability to work on - *In Alan's case this was presenting clearly and with clarity and giving his people a positive experience.*

Where possible, picture the venue where the event will take place. If you are unfamiliar with the venue, simply imagine it. *This was straightforward as Alan knew the venue and room layout.*

Keep your mind in the present, avoiding drifting into the past or away into a different event. Keep alert with everything in a clear focus. *This involved Alan practising his presentation mentally as well as physically.*

Employ all your five senses. What you can see, hear, feel, taste, and smell. This will heighten the value of the whole experience. Concentrate. *For Alan this means being aware of both himself and his people but also knowing what his evidence was for being in the Zone.*

Make sure that the experience is creating a genuine, physical, emotional response and 'feels right'. This is a vital part of ensuring that the maximum benefits are obtained. *The evidence for being in the Zone is often an emotional/physical one.*

Coaching For The Zone

Do the visualisation in an associated state, i.e. through your own eyes (in psychology this is called internal imagery). *For the Zone this is very important.*

Make the image as correct as possible. Help your mind and body to recognise, accept and respond to the highest levels of performance possible. This is part of the pre-programming for the future. *This will dramatically increase the chances of getting into the Zone in future.*

Ensure that everything in your visualisation is happening at normal speed. Sometimes it is possible to lose a sense of time when doing this. Therefore keep the process in real time. *Quite often Alan found things speeding up so it was important to practise this as much as possible.*

If you find it difficult to create a perfect picture, have a short break and come back to it. *A little, and often, works better than trying to do too much at one time.*

Repeat this process in a variety of different settings (e.g. when watching TV or while doing something else) in order to completely prepare for the moment when it is required. *This will help achieve the Zone at the right time and place and increase the chances of being able to repeat it.*

Session 2 – Sample Dialogue

Coach: So how important is this presentation Alan?

Alan: It's probably the most important thing I have done in years.

Coach: Why is that ?

Alan: Well, not only will I be judged on it… so will the performance of my team.

Coach: Okay, so how do you want to play it?

Alan: What do you mean?

Coach: Well, the purpose of the coaching is to help you progress and develop and we have already talked about your experiences of the Zone. So, do you want to pull all this together and use it to help you prepare and deliver the presentation?

Alan: Wow, that's a big one. I didn't see that one coming.

Coach: It's your shout, you don't have to do it this way. Let's talk through the implications.

Alan: Okay. [Discusses all the issues involved in using coaching for the Zone for the presentation]

Coach: So how do you feel about it now?

Alan: To be honest, scared to death, but I reckon I have to give it a go. It's too good an opportunity to miss.

Coach: Fine, lets unpick this a bit. How do you think your experiences of the Zone can help you in this situation?

Session 2 – Case Study – Sport

In this example the sports person was a female tennis player who had become a professional at a young age. She had a track record of success behind her but along the way had lost touch with, or alienated, her old friends without being able to replace them with her current peers.

So the reason she wanted to work with me, at the beginning, was not directly connected with her game but more about her social skills and how she could develop these in order to make new friends. I also realised that her experiences of the Zone, while being primarily tennis based, could be very helpful in getting her to tackle and break through with her social skills issue.

At our first session she had explained why she thought the situation had occurred but seemed unsure as to what to do. She did not seem really committed to tackling it. This observation only dawned on me after the session when I was reviewing it and writing up my notes, so I decided to mention it at session two.

On broaching the subject, which I did by pointing out it was my perception and my reasons for having the perception, she immediately became defensive and then, when I repeated my point, quite aggressive. I allowed her to vent her response and then asked her if this was how she reacted whenever she was told something she didn't like. She paused and then replied that it probably was and what was wrong with her responding like that? I replied that it wasn't necessarily a question of wrong or right but actually more likely to be about cause and effect. At this point she became more emotional and told me that she was aware she did it, but that it was a defence mechanism; in other words she 'got her attack in first' so that she then had, in her own mind, good reasons for not taking the point on-board and therefore not changing her behaviour.

At this point I asked her about her experiences of the Zone: whether she planned for it, did it just happen, what were the circumstances, what impact did it have on her and her performance, had she tried to repeat it? Finally I asked her if she had ever achieved the Zone in social circumstances? Much to her surprise she realised that it had occurred socially, but not very often and not for some time, and not in a planned-for way.

As a consequence of this discussion we then talked about how she could more effectively deal with new people and unexpected responses in the future. Initially she struggled with knowing what to do but she realised that if she could build on and develop the Zone this could help her deal with the issue. Her concern was becoming too mechanical and not being able to read a situation and having the skills to respond appropriately.

I reminded her that at our first session she had told me that one of her big strengths as a tennis player was being able to do exactly what we were now talking about (i.e. respond to the unexpected and deal with it effectively. That, she had said, was the key to her success). Her response was that the point was valid but specific to her playing tennis. I then said that if she could do it in the heat of battle on the tennis court there was no reason why she couldn't do it in other situations and that, as she had already proven, she did it away from tennis as well. Therefore we could build on these experiences of the Zone, (including both social and tennis experiences) to help her move forward.

She was initially sceptical about this but intrigued enough to keep a diary/log over the next month to note when these situations happened, how she responded, what resulted, and what she could have done differently - something she was already doing with regard to her tennis. This helped her to clarify her thoughts and actions, and to develop more considered and effective ways of dealing with the people and situations she faced.

Session 3

Session three is happening. How close to Alan's presentation should we schedule it?

Ideally, about 7 days beforehand.

Presumably, we kick off the session by reviewing the homework tasks Alan carried out?

Interestingly, I would not. I would actually spend 5 or 10 minutes reviewing the time between sessions (as we have done previously). It is likely that, although we are honing in on the presentation, the 10 minute recap will flush out lots of examples that will aid progress towards the presentation.

So, are you really saying – it is vital to do a recap at the beginning of every session? To not plough into the coaching session, even though you now 'know' the coachee.

Yes, that is correct. The coachee needs to see that although we are focusing on the presentation – and we will do everything to get him into the Zone for that – some of the other experiences will be relevant for Alan regarding either content or key points for the presentation. It also shows that although this session is primarily about the presentation, the presentation is part of a bigger picture (i.e. Alan's job and career). In addition, any experiences Alan has had regarding the Zone, either inside or outside work, could be really useful.

Okay, we have been through Alan's experiences over the previous few weeks. What is next?

The recap will inevitably have included some aspects of Alan's preparation for the presentation. So, we then specifically go into the details of the presentation (have things changed?), discuss the key objectives of the presentation, discuss how the individual will know the presentation will have been successful. Then, we will run through what Alan has done since the previous session in terms of striving for Zone experiences and developing his methodology of getting into the Zone. This obviously includes discussing the tasks that Alan agreed to do at Session Two.

Alan responds, "I tried to do visualization but I found it really difficult!" He looks you in the eye and asks, "Have I failed?"

Although visualization is invariably the best-known technique for the Zone – a lot of people feel that they struggle with it, and that they have failed with it. Some people will say, "I can't do it, I just can't visualise." The normal way to deal with this is to keep things light. Ask the coachee, "Do you ever dream? Do you ever day-dream? Can you picture the face of your partner or children, here and now?" "Describe your front room or your favourite beauty spot." It would be extremely unusual, at that point, for the coachee not to say, "Yes, I can do that." All the coach needs to do, now, is demonstrate that all of these are forms of visualisation and that they are completely natural and normal. Another way to do this is to ask Alan to describe his previous experience(s) of being in the Zone and what he could see while having the experience.

Alan admits that, maybe, developing his visualization skills was not quite as bad as he first made out. "The hard part was trying to visualise a future event although I was able, at times, to see myself in the presentation dealing with it - with confidence and with clarity. So, what should I do now with this image in my mind?"

Visualization, by itself, normally constitutes two things.

Firstly, replay (i.e. replaying a past experience – for many people this can mean a negative one!). Sometimes people struggle with a positive experiences because the picture appears more vague and blurred. At the same time, the coachee is incredibly sharp about negative images. That is an issue in its own right that can be dealt with through practice. In essence visualisation itself is not an issue, the issue is that the coachee is more affected and dominated by negative experiences and this explains a lot about the issues they have (and how they deal with them).

Secondly, visualization can also be about pre-play. The ability to replay is a fantastic skill but many coachees seem unaware of their ability to pre-play. Once the skill of being able to visualise a future event has been developed this can change everything and it can be a key factor for getting into the Zone on a more regular basis. For many coachees seeking to enter the Zone – becoming cognisant of pre-play and developing their pre-play skills will be the biggest breakthrough.

We have thoroughly reviewed the visualisation that Alan needed to do between sessions. We will not have another session before the big presentation – what should we now cover in anticipation of the big presentation?

We need to develop Alan's anchoring skills [see end of chapter]. We want to develop a cue (or signal or trigger) for Alan that will help him activate his replay or pre-play visualization – on demand, and under the pressure of performance.

In the final part of the session, we would look to talk through, plan for, and practice anchoring during the remainder of the time we have left. Alan would then continue this practice over the subsequent week in the run-up to the presentation.

Coaching For The Zone

As a coach, in the run-up to the presentation, would you make yourself available to Alan – should he need additional help?

Irrespective of context – sport, the business world, whatever – the bargain I strike with the coachee (which management or the coachee's organisation needs to be made aware of) is that I am available 24/7. That can mean email or telephone calls but it is not prescriptive. Between sessions, the coachee should be clear about what they are going away to do – but there is access available. I find, however, that if the sessions have been run properly the coachee will avail themselves a lot less than you might imagine. Some coaches avoid making themselves available outside session times because they think they are creating a need in the individual; although this is an obvious danger, in my experience it occurs very rarely.

As we draw Session 3 to a close, we have reviewed and tweaked (as needed) Visualization, and started work on Anchoring (which is practiced before the coachee leaves the session). Do we now send Alan away to practice these skills more?

We do. One of the key things that would normally emerge at this point is revisiting how the coachee will 'know' that the presentation or performance has gone well. Some of that can be very hard-edged in terms of scored outcomes or feedback (e.g. happy sheets) but, quite often, it is an internal feeling. People often 'know' when their performance has gone well by the round of applause they receive, or the number of questions asked.

For many people, the internal feeling is the most important. Sometimes this is literally the 'gut feel', sometimes it's a warm glow of satisfaction or a relaxed feel and being able to maintain eye contact with people. On a simplistic level it's rather like planning a journey with 'milestones' along the way and knowing you are doing the right things in order to arrive at your destination but then trusting yourself to get it right.

It is very important that Alan knows what his 'signals of success' are so that he can recognise when things are going well and - if there are issues - he knows what he has to do in order to change what he is doing. What confuses a lot of people is that these 'signals' are often 'soft' and only recognisable by the coachee. But I see this as an advantage as it means no one else knows what is happening internally with us.

Visualization (part II) and Anchoring

What will this task accomplish?

It will help Alan be, and feel, more prepared for his presentation. It involves Alan taking the skill of visualisation a stage further.

When should the coachee do it?

At least 3 to 4 times in the week building up to the performance/presentation; more if felt to be helpful.

How long should it take?

10 minutes

Instructions for the Coachee

This is built upon the more structured visualisation that Alan is already familiar with and involves him taking the skill of visualisation a stage further. We want Alan to have an image of himself performing excellently, dealing appropriately with any problems (e.g. difficult questions that occur), feeling he is achieving his outcomes and milestones, being able to 'self coach' as he goes along in a balanced purposeful way. Some useful questions at this point, for Alan to work through, are:

- What is my desired outcome for this stage of the preparation?
- How will I know that I have achieved my outcome for this stage?
- What specific techniques am I working on as part of my preparation (e.g. visualisation, anchoring, etc.)
- Can I use my previous experiences of being in the Zone to help me prepare?
- How do I know that I am in the Zone (i.e. what is my evidence?)

Note. There is a degree of repetition and overlap in doing this but it helps Alan/the coachee embed the key ingredients for getting in the Zone.

Anchoring

Purpose

To enable the coachee to optimise a resourceful state whenever they need it.

Time

10 minutes per day

Instructions for the Coachee

1. Identify a resource state you want (either on a more regular basis or for specific moments).
2. Find a specific occasion in your life when you had this resource. If you cannot do this - imagine it. Alternatively, think of someone else you have seen exhibit it.
3. Go back to that moment. Relive the state you were in and remember what you could see, hear, feel, smell and taste. Then come back to the here and now and decide what anchors you want - to recreate that resourceful feeling. This should be a combination of the five senses (e.g. a specific visual image, a specific word or phrase, a specific gesture or touch such as touching the face, pulling an ear lobe). This is your anchor.
4. In your mind's eye put yourself fully back into the resource state you want. See what you could see, hear, feel, smell and taste and be fully in touch with your body and feelings. If there is a sequence of events - relive them in that sequence. If there is a certain body position or aspect to your physiology - re-acquire that.
5. Just as the resourceful feeling is fully coming together and peaking, connect up (fire) your anchor (i.e. see your image, hear/say your word or phrase, make your gesture, etc.). Doing this at the peak moment will create your anchor.
6. Do this five or six times to really build the connections.
7. Test the anchor. Repeat the process. Test that you can achieve the resourceful state at will.
8. Mentally rehearse your anchor before the time that you want to be able to operate it.
9. Use the anchor at the time you require it.

Note

The process of building and using resource anchors is a generative process (i.e.

they become easier the more you use them).

Putting an anchor in place then firing it six months later might work but success is much greater with practice.

Firing anchors at the moment you need them is very powerful. You can have as many anchors as you need for a situation.

Further Note

Anchors are very important in helping to achieve the Zone.

Anchors can be used at any of the coaching sessions. In this example they were introduced at Session Three because of Alan's requirements.

Session 3 – Sample Dialogue

Coach: When you are doing something like an important presentation, or something that really matters to you, how do you know you are getting it right?

Alan: On one level that sounds like a dumb question because it should be obvious, on another level I'm not sure I know the answer.

Coach: Give it a go.

Alan: Well there's the normal things like applause, questions, the Happy Sheets at the end, but I'm not sure that's what you mean.

Coach: They are obviously important but they tend to be external indicators. For you and the Zone I'm interested in how you know *inside* that it is going well and working for you. If it helps I call these your 'signals of success'.

Alan: Do you mean things like gut feel or something like that?

Coach: Absolutely, that's a classic one, but it could be a physical sense, or knowing your mind is clear, smiling, engaging with the audience rather than talking at them; there are loads of things potentially. The skill is to clarify yours so that you know you are getting it right and, if for some reason you aren't getting it right, you can modify what you are doing.

Alan: This sounds crucial, let me give it some thought.

Coach: Okay, think back to some previous examples of when you were in the Zone but don't just think about work and presentations, think about any experiences... how did you know you were getting it right.

Session 3 – Case Study – Sport

This was an unusual situation in that the sports person involved, a professional cricketer, sought help when, as far as everyone else was concerned, everything was going well. In truth, this is the most appropriate time to work with someone like me, however it is much more normal to not seek help at this point either because the person believes top level performance will continue, or they are concerned that by analysing good performance somehow they will lose it. This can be particularly true of the Zone, something that seems illogical and counter intuitive, but it happens a lot.

The situation was that the player had spent a long time getting into the First Team, even though they had performed well at every level they had played. On getting into the First Team good performances had continued and they were now accepted as being a genuine member of the squad and team, which was why no one realised there was an issue.

I had worked with the player over a two year period and knew that while he was 100% committed to his career he had always held deeply hidden doubts about his true ability; this is where his skill to get into the Zone on a regular basis had proven so helpful. However, it was obvious that to him the issue of his 'true' ability was still there.

We had our usual pre-season session and then a second one about a month into the season. At this session he said that while his form was very good he was worrying about it, losing sleep, and bothered that - inevitably - this would catch up with him and his form would be affected.

Rather than leap into action and offer suggestions, I asked him to talk me through some of his performances and the processes he was currently using. His response was that I already knew this because we had worked on them together. I pointed out that this was indeed the case but that I thought it would be both helpful and revealing to unpick them. I also asked him to clarify what the one key issue he wanted to tackle was. His response was that his biggest issue was his sleep problems. I asked him if he had tried any of the techniques he used to mentally prepare for the Zone to aid the sleep problem, and he said he hadn't ever thought of it. I suggested we spend some time doing this and see what came out of it.

We spent about 40 minutes doing this and the main points to emerge were that a combination of visualisation and a willingness to try new things were most helpful to him. I then asked him whether there was a pattern to when and what woke him up, and how he tried to get back to sleep. He replied that he went out like a light but woke up in the middle of the night with his mind on fire and had great difficulty in getting back to sleep.

I asked him if he thought having some processes, based upon the ones he used to help his cricket performances would help. He thought that they could but was bothered that if they didn't work they would impact negatively on the ones he was using for his cricket. I pointed out that although based on the same processes they would be unique and specific to his sleep issue and would not adversely affect his cricket.

The outcome of session three was that we developed a visualisation to help him go to sleep, a different one should he wake in the night, and combined them with a breathing/calming exercise to use while playing.

He was then able to prove to himself that he could solve the problem and that the Zone could be used to 'switch off' as well as 'switch on'.

Session 4

Session 4 begins, and Alan reports that the presentation went well; "better than expected" in his own words. Feedback was good. Alan wants to know where he can take visualization and anchoring further.

Inevitably, we will require a little bit more of a detailed debrief. What you tend to get, at this point, is a general view - which is a little subjective - which won't help Alan learn and embed what he has achieved.

First, we should get Alan to talk through his presentation – this does not mean re-presenting the whole presentation. Rather it means talking through what he remembers of the presentation. This is really important with anyone trying to get into the Zone because, although they will likely find the process hard, it will be immensely beneficial - it will help them recreate the key skills and actions they *actually used* and enable them to recreate them on future occasions. Moments will arise such as [Alan:] "Oh, I didn't think that was very important at the time, but things changed when the MD asked me that particular question." So, in essence, this detailed more probing debrief enables us to get into better specifics of what worked, and what did not work. A detailed discussion will help Alan think through not only his own experiences and reactions, but also their impact on other people and how best he can make use of them to help become a more effective Manager.

Moving towards the end of the session, we will be talking about how to embed the things that went well, so they can be repeated. We want to make the Zone a repeatable experience. Whilst positive points are addressed, it is also important to get a handle on the parts that went less well. We want Alan to help identify - based on his own experience of the coaching program so far - what he thinks he could have done differently, better, more of, and less of.

Okay, we have done a thorough debrief. Where do we now take this session; there is no big presentation coming up… Alan is back to his day-to-day routine.

Funnily enough, this is *as important* (if not more important) as when preparing for the presentation. If the Zone is only ever seen as getting through the presentation or other 'big events' then we are not actually helping Alan. We need to now look at what is coming up – even if it may be seen as normal or run-of-the-mill. There will be more than enough opportunities to take what Alan has learned from his presentation and apply it to his day-to-day activities.

Do we identify day-to-day activities (that Alan wishes to improve) and make a list, or do we identify more generic activities?

In my experience, taking the big experience which was tangible and specific, and finding similar things that are smaller (in a way) can be a good way to proceed although it depends on the needs of the client.

The next stage could be about being effective in meetings, or carrying out effective appraisals, for example. However, I would normally seek to carry on the 'specificity' of what we have already done because that is what will best embed appropriate techniques in the coachee and help them more in the future.

Alan has identified, during the debrief, a number of smaller areas that he would like to focus on. One of these is the end of quarter, where he would like to get his house in order. Another one is expanding the team (recruitment). Another one is an IT upgrade that needs implementing. Three significant, but not career defining, moments have been identified. How do we go about these three things?

The first thing to discuss is priorities. And those priorities might be for the department or organization, they might be for the individual, or the team.

Allow the coachee to choose the pecking order for each of the identified areas, bearing in mind that this must take account of the factors mentioned above. Translate that back into the experience of the presentation and ask Alan what aspects / skills (even though there is a different context) he can transfer or apply to the new areas. Then, repeat the processes of visualization and anchoring for these new areas. This will also help propagate Alan's interest in visualisation and anchoring.

It is at this point that we would likely be getting into new techniques because although Alan likes the visualisation and anchoring techniques it is important that (in order to help him in the future) he knows how to use other relevant techniques. For example, with an appraisal – we will be examining how Alan interacts with other people. Or Alan's personal organisation. We will then use relevant techniques for these activities.

With the session coming to a close, and three new areas for performance improvement identified, is there a new technique you plan to send Alan away to work on?

One of the most obvious ones, which will nearly always crop up (and in Alan's context it is now) is a technique of affirmation. Many people have the 'inner voice' (the self-critic) which is often critical and negative and not empowering. The purpose, in sport or any other context, is not to be positive for the sake of it but to take a previous experience that has gone well (which maybe was not expected to have gone well) and create affirmations for other experiences coming up.

And how does the technique of affirmation link into our overall aim of coaching the Zone?

What we are trying to help Alan achieve is a structured framework he can use in order to get into the Zone. Structured does not mean prescriptive, however, and Alan will need a number of tools and techniques in order to give him the flexibility to be able to respond to a variety of circumstances. Affirmations are a well-known and well-used approach and an important option to help any coachee who is looking to improve their performance and get into the Zone more regularly.

41

*[Between Sessions, the Coach and Alan have agreed
that Alan will complete the following Task]*

Affirmation

What will this task accomplish?

It will equip Alan with another practical technique to help him get into the Zone.

When should the coachee do it?

Affirmations can be practised on a regular basis but work best when based on a specific event.

How long should it take?

5 – 10 minutes, and as many times per day as relevant and helpful.

Instructions for the Coachee

Think of a forthcoming event that you are feeling nervous or concerned about.

Think about how you would express that nervousness or concern e.g. 'I am no good at giving presentations' or 'I always feel uncomfortable when meeting new people' or 'If this goes wrong it will look bad on me'.

Go back to previous experiences of this type of event and remember the parts of it you did well or which were successful. This is extremely important even if the event was in a different context (e.g. meeting people outside work).

Develop and commit to a phrase that you can use to substitute for the negative phrase whenever you need to (e.g. 'I get good feedback for my presentations' or 'When I meet people for the first time they seem to like me' or 'what can I do to make this go well for me?')

Note. Affirmations are not just mindless repetitions of 'positive thinking' which are not based on reality. They are considered views which can be used to help the coachee overcome previous blockages or difficulties.

It also possible to anchor the affirmation for future use. This is an example of techniques mapping over each other - in order to improve the chances of getting into the Zone in the future.

Session 4 – Sample Dialogue

This sample dialogue takes place as part of the debrief conversation into Alan's presentation.

Coach: So, overall, you feel the presentation went well?

Alan: Yes, much better than I might have hoped.

Coach: What makes you feel that?

Alan: A number of things really. The atmosphere during the presentation, the number of questions I got and answered, plus the comments afterwards.

Coach: Okay, let's take them one at a time. What do you mean by the atmosphere?

Alan: Everyone was very relaxed and responsive.

Coach: Including you?

Alan: Well yes, I suppose so. I remember looking round the room and feeling that I was actually enjoying it.

Coach: How do you think you achieved this?

Alan: I feel the preparation helped, although - thinking about it - I don't just mean the preparation regarding the content, I would have done that anyway. I mean the preparation for myself.

Coach: Such as?

Alan: Well, the visualisation helped, but it was mainly the anchoring that felt the most useful.

Coach: Why do you think that was?

Alan: It made me feel like I could deal with anything, but not in an arrogant way. It was more like being liberated.

Coach: How do you think you can take this forward?

Alan: There are lots of other areas of my work and life where it would be really useful.

Coach: Okay, let's note down some of those areas then we can go through the other things that went well in the presentation, then pull it all together and decide how best to move forward.

Session 4 – Case Study – Sport

The situation involved in this Case Study involved someone coming to the end of their sporting career as a highly successful athlete. My client had given all her time and thoughts to achieving her goals, with virtually no thought for what could happen next. At the same time as she was coming to the end of her career she sustained an injury which stopped it completely. As a consequence she felt that there was 'unfinished business' that, due to the injury, would now remain unfinished.

We had worked together at various points in her career but she had always done little bits, felt she had solved a short term issue and stopped and moved on – until the next issue arose. Therefore, during the first three sessions, I worked through what she had achieved in her career, how she had achieved it, what she had learnt from it, and how she could apply all this in order to move forward. In particular, I made the point that while she could stop any time I felt that this needed to be a medium- to long-term approach, something she said yes to, but without seeming entirely convinced.

As part of the process in the first three sessions I had tasked her to develop a list of the skills, experiences, attitudes, problems overcome, and lessons learnt that she thought would be helpful to help her create her future; included in this were her experiences of the Zone. Like most sports people she tended to only see her experiences as relevant within the narrow application of her sport and although we had worked on the Zone outside her sport and she had good experiences of it she still didn't see all the connections.

Therefore I decided to use session four for anything she wanted to deal with but specifically to focus on breaking through this self-created barrier. In preparing for this I realised that just talking things through, although important, would only partially change things, as this had been our standard approach before. We needed to use her experiences of the Zone to give her more confidence that she could move forward and achieve what she wanted after, and possibly outside, her sport.

She was very familiar with visualisation and had found it really powerful for her athletics so I decided to build on this but add in helping her to move more 'into the future' rather than focus on the past. Additional techniques were anchoring and affirmation to enable her to be aware of the past but, more importantly, to help her create her own future. At this point I realised that although anchoring and affirmations are two of the most effective techniques for getting into the Zone, we had not used either in our previous work together.

This approach proved to be a major breakthrough as it enabled my client to start to see the future she wanted, that this future was realistic, and that she could achieve it (because she saw what she could do, rather than what she couldn't). This mindset was the key to her success with the Zone. Following our work together, my client started to speak at conferences, allowed the media to interview her, built on her networking skills, set up her own consultancy, and wrote articles for journals and magazines that allowed her to develop her skills and confidence and public profile.

Session 5

Alan comes in and, straightaway, reports that, of the three areas identified in session 4, two have gone well but he is really struggling with the IT upgrade; specifically that he is grappling to manage something he does not understand (he is not IT-literate) and the people developing the upgrade know far more than he does.

Although Alan has raised this issue immediately, I would stick with the game plan of doing a quick review of what has been done between sessions. Although the IT upgrade will be part of that review, we need to take a balanced view – and that involves the other two areas that were agreed. This does not mean we ignore the IT issue, it simply means we put it into proper perspective.

As we debrief on the IT integration, the coach is likely to need to ask a lot of questions and establish exactly what has happened.

Looking at this particular example, it is likely that Alan has been blinded by his lack of technical skill. If that is the case – and it is for Alan to determine this, not the coach – it is worth pointing out that Alan is actually using coaching to improve the performance of his IT team. He may not realise it, or be doing it overtly, but everything he does regarding his people has some impact on their performance, even though it may not be technical. Accordingly, whilst being an expert in the field can be an advantage, it is not necessarily the advantage that many people think. If an expert ends up coaching someone else, they often end up perpetuating their own experiences and views of how to progress matters without actually achieving the goal of developing their people.

Coaching For The Zone

We can ask Alan what skills he might have used, based on the coaching experience (and the Zone as well) in order not to let those IT-related situations develop.

It feels, in this context, as though the Zone is less relevant than broader 'coaching'. Is there any way we can integrate the Zone into what we are trying to accomplish here?

Almost certainly there will be. The important thing here is to deal with Alan's specific situation through coaching whilst keeping the Zone 'there' as a place we want to go. However, one of the proving points for the Zone is Alan's ability to get into the Zone in any situation where it would be helpful and this situation may be one of those.

It is critical though, at this stage, that any coaching is specific to the situation Alan is facing, otherwise in the end it will lack validity and long term impact. This can facilitate Alan's experiences of the Zone which he might be able to share with his people. Of course, Alan might say it is not required for his IT people to be 'in the Zone' all the time in order to be effective. In other words, the Zone might be a desirable here, not an essential.

So, when coaching for the Zone, the important thing is remember that you are coaching first and foremost, and sometimes have to take a step away in order to coach more immediate challenges?

Yes. Deal with the issue or problem that the coachee is facing. It is about how the coach unpicks this issue, and helps the coachee think it through, which allows the coach to create the bridge to work towards the Zone.

We are halfway through session 5, and Alan has visibly relaxed about his IT problem. Now, there is an opportunity to help Alan with a new element of personal Zone development. What do you do?

I would aim for Alan to draw connections between his experiences of the Zone and the situation he is facing, and make the point that his experience of the Zone may not be the same as anyone else's. Other people's experiences will be based

48

on their working criteria and context – which may be very different. As Alan is a manager, I would be helping Alan to sow the seeds as to what he could do to manage his situation - whilst bearing in mind his desire to be able to get into the Zone more regularly.

The Session is closing. What task would you like Alan to go away with?

I would ask Alan to keep the Zone as a big picture item, but think specifically – based on his knowledge as a manager and his experience of being coached – what he could do to embed the performance of his IT team and his other people. And what specific steps he would need to take.

Would this be a written document?

It could be. It could be verbal, or it might be one of those occasions (which I would not do all of the time) when you ask the coachee to go away, reflect, then send you a one/two page email summarising what was asked of the coachee.

Would you also ask Alan to continue visualisations, affirmations, and anchoring?

Yes. All of those as appropriate. As we have mentioned previously, Alan should not see these skills in the narrow context of the presentation. He needs to be able to learn from it, and transfer it, and apply it in other contexts. That is also the reason why we are introducing Controlled Breathing at this stage.

[Between Sessions, the Coach and Alan have agreed
that Alan will complete the following Task]

Review of Zone Experiences

What will this task accomplish ?

It will help Alan to think through his own experiences of the Zone and how he goes about managing his people. It is vital that Alan can do this without being prompted by the questions the coach is asking him. It will also help him think through his own experiences.

When should the coach use it?

This is one of those tools that can be used at any time but might never be used at all. I tend to use this quite a lot but choose the moments/situations where I believe it will be most helpful.

How long should it take?

Because it is mainly used as an occasional tool it requires half an hour to an hour to do, initially, plus time for whatever additional thoughts Alan has later. It may also be one of those times when you ask the coachee to email their response to you by a given date so you have read it before the next session.

Instructions for the coachee

Because the purpose for doing this exercise is a) to get the coachee to think through their own experiences and b) to help them think through how they could apply them, I would not be too prescriptive by providing a set of questions. The coachee has now attended five sessions so knows how the coach approaches situations so I would leave it to them to structure their own thoughts. If they want further guidance they can always make contact .

The one point I would make is that the notes should not be more than two pages long.

Controlled Breathing

What this activity will achieve

When getting into the Zone and (also) carrying out the activities covered in this book it is vital to have a clear mind. Focused, controlled, deep breathing is an effective means of achieving this. Controlled breathing will help the coachee to remain calm under pressure in order to be able to focus and concentrate.

Time required

10 minutes every day for a week.

- a. Put one hand on your chest and the other on your stomach
- b. Breathe in through your nose. The hand on your stomach should rise. The hand on your chest should rise very little. *Count in, two three, four*
- c. Exhale through your mouth pushing out as much air as you can, while contracting your abdominal muscles. The hand on your stomach should move in as you exhale, but your other hand should not move much. *Count out, two, three, four.*
- d. Breathe in through your nose ....*in, two, three, four*
- e. Exhale through your mouth......*out ,two, three, four*
- f. *In, two, three, four*
- g. *Out, two, three, four*

Session 5 – Sample Dialogue

This Sample Dialogue is part of the conversation the coach and Alan have regarding Alan's issues in dealing with IT.

Coach: Alan, I get the feeling that you are working around the IT situation without really tackling it; is this an accurate view on my part?

Alan: Absolutely, I know I am doing it but don't know what else to do.

Coach: Why do you think this is happening?

Alan: I think the main reason is that they know much more about the day-to-day aspects of IT than I do.

Coach: Well that's hardly a surprise, that's their job; that's why they are there. Your job is to be their manager and help them move forward both with their projects and their development.

Alan: I suppose so but surely I should know what they know?

Coach: Why?

Alan: So I can make sure they are doing it right? [Alan then pauses, thinking, the coach stays silent while Alan is thinking] That doesn't sound right, surely being a manager involves more than just checking up on people.

Coach: Like how?

Alan: Well as you say, running the team, dealing with higher management, developing people, running the budget, doing appraisals, going to meetings and loads of other things.

Coach: Right, so how can you do all of the things you are actually being paid to do, if you are spending all your time checking people's work? How do you think you can move more towards this management role?

Alan: One of the things I have noticed about how you deal with me is that you ask me loads of questions to get me to think through my own experiences and consider how best to move forward.

Coach: So? (Laughs)

Alan: (Laughs) There you go again. Actually I found it really annoying at the beginning but I think I've worked out why you do it.

Coach: (Grinning) Why is that?

Alan: Well, if we take the Zone, for example, you made me dig really deep so that I found out for myself whether I had been in the Zone and how best I could repeat the experience on a more regular basis.

Coach: So how does that help you with the Zone, and your people, and their projects?

Alan: As it is obvious that *you* don't really understand much about IT, and even though you know about the Zone - you didn't tell me about it too much. You let me tell you and then used that to move forward, so I guess I could do that with my people.

Coach: How could you start doing that?

[The conversation then moves on as to how best Alan can move forward.]

Session 5 – Case Study – Sport

In the first four sessions with an international Rugby Player we had covered issues such as building confidence, repeating high levels of performance, and coming back from injury. The player had been very open, receptive to ideas, and willing to try things out. As part of this we had established his processes for the Zone and he seemed very comfortable with this.

However, I always had the nagging feeling that there was something we weren't getting to (but I couldn't work out if I was right or wrong in this perception). With some people I would come straight out and ask them, making the point that it was just a perception; however, in this case, my instinct was not to do that. So on the basis of only dealing with what was happening (and therefore concrete) I decided to keep going with what we were doing.

However, part way through the fifth session, my client seemed to be distracted and vague about what we were discussing - so I asked him if everything was okay. He started to talk about some random aspects of his career and his non-verbal communication became more demonstrative (i.e. his tone of voice, speed of speech, and gestures became more overt). After a few minutes, while I just let him talk, he said "This is probably not very important but…" Often phrases like this are verbal markers that the *really* important point is just about to emerge (if we let it).

This was one of those moments when the old adage 'say nothing and continue to listen' applied so I nodded and waited to see what (if anything) would emerge. To my total surprise he started to talk about how long it had taken him to feel that he fitted into the international dressing room and stated that it was not until he was playing his 20th international that he started to feel comfortable. He also said that it was the work we had done on the Zone that had allowed him to focus on *getting himself right* rather than being distracted by his worries.

As we discussed the background to this situation I saw a completely different side to him, still a really good person but someone who was subject to lots of insecurities. Through the conversation it emerged that this issue had affected him in lots of previous situations e.g. changing schools and clubs, meeting new people, and elsewhere.

As we probed further I asked him if something had ever gone wrong or he had failed in any of these situations. He thought long and hard and his surprise was obvious when he realised he had handled and come through a large number of such situations successfully. At this point I asked him to talk me through two or three of them asking him to see if he felt there were any effective patterns he was using, even if he didn't realise at the time. Again, unprompted, he mentioned the Zone even though he hadn't realised at the time that it was the Zone or that he was actually living the Zone.

Through this conversation he was able to elicit that there were a number of key things he did each time (e.g. not push himself forward, ask lots of questions, create rapport, follow up on conversations, show animated interest). We were then able to turn these into a set of affirmations which he could then use on future occasions when required. These built on the affirmations he used for his rugby.

One fascinating point about this session was that the issue of 'fitting in' cropped up after he had come through the problem situation (at this stage he was an established international player). Further discussions, at later sessions, revealed that although he had clearly overcome the problem of fitting in with his international teammates, he hadn't realised it, and still carried the issue around with him. He felt that it affected both his performance, and him as a person, in spite of the evidence to the contrary. Revealing this and his subsequent realisation that it was a self-created issue, based on perception not fact, was a massively liberating experience for him.

Session 6

Alan is back for session 6 and the regular review has taken place. The IT problem, whilst better, has not been fully resolved. Alan feels out of his depth and has little confidence in his ability to manage the project.

Ask questions to establish the true cause of any problem rather than Alan's perceptions of it. Go back to what Alan was trying to achieve, what techniques he has tried, and which techniques have worked (and which have not). Probe into these and establish *reasons* why some things have worked and some have not. Look for patterns and themes as these may provide the best ways to move forward.

Then move on, and get Alan to look at some of the key blocks. Ascertain whether the key blocks are his blocks, or whether they are technical blocks involving the project. If they are his blocks these can be dealt with through the coaching process; remind him of his previous experiences of getting things right and being in the Zone. If they are technical blocks establish who actually has the answer/expertise, how to get it, and how to share it with those others that need it. Remind Alan that, at session five, he had realised that he didn't need to have all the technical expertise himself, that his job was to manage the people and the project.

Coaching For The Zone

Alan suggests the problem is 'dealing with other people'. The IT team – because he has no technical understanding – just don't seem to take him seriously. Alan feels the issue is one of relationships.

Alan's view on the world is a self-limiting one which, of course, is not unusual. If it is going to impact on Alan it's as well that it has cropped up during the coaching. It sounds as though Alan is operating on a set of self-limiting beliefs and building some safety walls around himself (comfort zones) which ironically - in the end - actually create discomfort. Equally, Alan is at the point (as many managers will experience) where he has enjoyed some experience that the Zone is working for him (in terms of optimizing his own personal performance) but has now encountered the classic stumbling block of trying to do something with other people!

So, we should look back specifically at the techniques already developed, and ask what skills (and the development of said skills) would help Alan re-enter the Zone in these problem circumstances. These skills might include: influencing people, dealing with self-limiting beliefs, problem solving, decision making, creating rapport, giving and seeking feedback, clarifying objectives.

But, how would the Zone manifest itself with these particular skills? Would Alan simply become more fluid and confident in what he is doing (the idea of things becoming effortless while still performing to a high level)?

Although this can sound vague, Alan may not realise (at the time) that he is (sometimes) already in the Zone when working with his people. It may be when he is driving home in the evening that he realises that he has overcome an issue, or accelerated the project, or that the mood in a team meeting was much better, that Alan sees that what he did was automatic and Zone-like. In essence, Alan is responding appropriately but not consciously thinking about it. These are examples of what is called 'unconscious competence' but because Alan is focussing on the negatives he does not realise these positive examples are occurring.

At this point the pattern of reviewing the past in order to move forward is well established and should come naturally to Alan, so he should only need prompting and reminding of how it works. The tricky thing for the coach is not to fall into the trap of just telling Alan he is doing some good things, and how he has examples of being effective and of being in the Zone, but to help Alan find them for himself.

Having said that it also important to help Alan establish that his future actions will add to his armoury of experiences, successes, tools and techniques. Also that any blips and failures will equally help him move forward; that failure is a part of learning and changing behaviour, provided that he learns from them.

This is session six of an expected eight-part programme. Is this a good point for the coach to start identifying the end of the programme, and providing Alan with ownership for afterwards?

It is absolutely vital that this done, yes. But it does come with dangers and restrictions.

We don't want the coachee to think 'it's all over' and take their foot off the gas. Equally, they have some real-life problems, now, that they want help with. The best way to embed the Zone, and convince a client of the value of coaching, is to help the coachee tackle real-life issues. However, we would not be doing justice to the process if the coachee was not (at least) turning his/her mind towards self-ownership and self-development for after the eighth session. It is not unusual for the coachee to either revert to a 'I won't be able to do this by myself' mode, or go completely the other way and believe that they can handle anything.

So would we plan to map out sessions seven and eight at this point, or speak more broadly with Alan about what he wants to accomplish?

I would be saying to Alan: "What are the things we want to accomplish by the end of session eight?", in order to develop self-ownership and the transfer of accountability and responsibility.

I would also encourage him to be thinking about the processes he has worked on/developed and how he intends to further develop them. In other words I would want Alan to be thinking about processes and not drift too far into concepts. However we achieve that along the way, balanced with Alan's specific IT issue, is for us to decide and agree. We can agree the content and the approach between ourselves with the proviso that, by the end of session eight, we know where we need to be.

Coaching For The Zone

With session six drawing to a close, we need to send Alan away to focus on a task. Having identified various skills during the review that could be improved – what are you going to ask Alan to go away and do?

I would ask Alan to revisit his skillset and rate where he thinks he is on a scale (e.g. 0-10) and get him to consider where he wants to be by the end of session eight. It is not necessarily the case that he needs to be at 10 to enter the Zone.

Accordingly, having completed this task, during session seven, we can plan for skills improvement. Although there are only to be two more sessions there are still two months of time involved and they should be used to the maximum benefit. It is vital that Alan uses the time between the sessions as effectively as possible.

It feels like you are asking Alan to start driving the programme himself.

Correct. I like to think, if I have been successful (particularly in the context of the Zone) that Alan has been driving it anyway. He may not have quite realised it, of course.

It is a real compliment to the coach when the coachee smiles at the end of the session or programme and says, "I'm not really quite sure what you have done, and I've really got benefit from it, but I think I've done all the work." Removing the ego of the coach from that (and bearing in mind what the Zone is) – I would take that as possibly the ultimate compliment.

*[Between Sessions, the Coach and Alan have agreed
that Alan will complete the following Task]*

Alan will go back to his original set of skills/ issues he wanted to deal with, plus any that have occurred along the way.

He will, on a scale of 0-10, decide where he is now and where he wants to be in two months' time at the end of the programme. I would avoid complicating this by trying to agree definitions for each part of the scale; I would leave this to Alan's judgement for us to discuss at session seven.

I would also ask him to consider what processes he has used, which have worked, which have not, and what further support he requires before the end of session eight.

Centering

Purpose

Centering as a skill builds on the Breathing Activity covered in Session 5 and allows the coachee to take charge of their mind and body at key moments. Centering will allow the coachee to focus all their attention and energy on the issue they are dealing with at that moment (e.g. getting in to the Zone).

Time

10 minutes every day for a week – then on a regular basis.

   a. Stand with your feet apart and knees bent slightly with your weight evenly distributed between your two feet. This is about finding your physical centre of gravity which is normally just below your waist. Remember where your centre is – as this part of your body stabilises you.
   b. Relax the neck and shoulders with your mouth slightly open to reduce the tension in your jaw muscles.
   c. Breathe in through your nose and push your stomach out. As you do so, focus on two things: your stomach moving out, and maintaining the relaxation in your neck and shoulders.

    d.   Exhale slowly through your mouth and feel your stomach muscles relaxing and your body pressing down to the ground.

    e.   Repeat this process five more times.

    f.   Focus on the feelings of relaxation.

Session 6 – Sample Dialogue

Coach: Alan, I get the sense that you feel you have achieved a lot, but that it feels all jumbled up and you don't really feel in control of it all.

Alan: That's pretty much it. To be honest I expected to feel better about it all by now and have some clear evidence that I was getting somewhere.

Coach: Okay. Go on.

Alan: Well I expected to be clearer about what I needed to do to get myself (and others) into the Zone.

Coach: It may not be any consolation but this normally happens at some point, and this happens to be yours. Let's see what we can do about it.

Alan: Great, where do we start ?

Coach: Why don't we revisit some of the experiences you have had of the Zone; look at the techniques you have tried, establish which ones worked for you under what circumstances, and then develop a *framework* for you to apply for the future.

Alan: Excellent, let's do that.

Coach: Remember, it is your experiences we are reviewing, not my interpretation of them so you must lead the discussion and make sure you are getting 'what you want' out of it.

Alan: Fair enough. Which experience should we start with?

Coach: You choose…

Session 6 – Case Study – Sport

The background to this case study revolved around a young footballer who had been taken on by a professional club and put into their academy. He had run into difficulties settling in and was thinking of dropping out and giving up.

I had seen him on five previous occasions and, unusually in a coaching situation, was seeing him fortnightly rather than at longer intervals due to his age and the immediacy of the situation. During the previous situations we had revisited his experiences of being in the Zone and agreed a set of activities for him to work on in order to achieve it more often.

My client was someone who only saw the Zone in the context of sport and, initially, was reluctant to work on it in other situations. What finally persuaded him was the realisation that if he didn't do something he would be out of football, something he had wanted for his whole life.

In working with him on his approaches to the Zone it became apparent that when working on his football he was highly kinaesthetic (i.e. aware of his feelings and emotions and very much in touch with himself). However, when dealing with the rest of his life he tended to be more auditory and logical, not trusting his feelings and instincts. The approach we therefore adopted was to a) to use similar approaches to getting into the Zone in sport and the rest of his life, but b) to ensure that in doing this he was using his feelings and instincts.

In discussing these approaches with my client he became very animated and passionate about how much football meant to him and how his view of himself as a person was affected by being a footballer. As part of this I asked him if it was because of football in itself, or, because it meant he was doing something that fulfilled him (because it meant something important to him). In doing so, I realised this was quite a big question for someone so young, but both my instinct and judgement told me it was the right question at the right time.

We then spent ten minutes discussing his response which, in essence, was that it was more about him as a person making the most of his skills and being able to know he had given everything he could. Then we revisited his actions to help him achieve this.

This approach enabled the young footballer to deal with the wider aspects of becoming a professional footballer but also, interestingly, impacted on his football as he became able to not only to take the Zone from football into the rest of his life but also *the other way around.*

> *Mediocrity knows nothing higher than itself,*
> *but talent instantly recognises genius.*

Sir Arthur Conan Doyle

Session 7 has begun and, as always, the recap has been carried out. Alan has identified a number of areas that need strengthening but one in particular is prominent. Decision making. Alan feels he is slow, and not very effective in making the right decisions. What can we do here?

One of the key things is to determine what blocks are in place that are stopping Alan from making decisions. One particular block, for example, could be something like 'losing face'. Perhaps Alan holds off making decisions because he fears he might make the wrong decision which will damage his credibility/others' views of him? Quite often, a lack of decision making won't be about the technical content of the decision (although the coachee may say it is). This is partly because it can be difficult to acknowledge discomfort when making decisions because everyone expects people to be able to make them. After all, everyone is an expert on other peoples' issues and decisions!

In turn, the discussion with Alan needs to address the perceived benefits of making decisions more sharply/more quickly (and how that would affect Alan entering the Zone). Furthermore, a discussion can be held that examines what previously covered techniques can be used. What evidence would convince Alan that his decision making has improved? Does Alan have the opportunity to practice his decision making on smaller or bigger decisions over the next few weeks?

Coaching For The Zone

Alan asks a question. "What would decision making, in the Zone, feel like?"

It would feel like Alan was not aware of making a decision (i.e. it would happen automatically). All the trauma of making a decision would not be there. On reflection, Alan would realise, 'I made that decision entirely naturally, entirely intuitively, without conscious thought.' Having analysed the outcome, Alan would realise that he would not have been able to come up with a better decision even if he had taken longer and thought about it more, and analysed the data in great detail.

Alan says that is great 'in theory', but how can he now work towards creating a better state of decision making?

Alan, of course, is quite right! It is true that when 'in the Zone' decision making becomes automatic and unconscious, however in the cold light of day this can sound woolly and vague. Remember this is session seven so, as the coach, you now know Alan really well and will have a number of examples he will have previously provided that can now be referred to. As with the practice referenced below, these examples can be from any context or situation, they don't have to be from exactly the same situations. In other words there will be some examples of Alan already demonstrating that he can make good decisions.

The danger here is that we make the process sound over-elaborate. Really it is based on recognising the blocks that need to be removed to create a sense of freedom. So decision making in the Zone, and often outside it, is often not about putting extra skills/steps in, but about removing some of the blockages - most of which are in the client's head. Therefore Alan now needs to practice his decision making and learn to trust himself more when doing so.

This practice need not solely be to do with work. As a coach, you should ask Alan whether decision making is also a problem outside work and whether there are opportunities to practice outside work.

Alan scratches his head and looks the coach square in the eyes. "Isn't good decision making just about confidence?" he asks. "Isn't it about taking a decision that might, or might not, be wrong, and living with the consequences?"

The answer is yes, but you have to look at the context of the consequences. Decision making for a hobby could be very different to decision making at work. So, yes, it is a confidence thing. But confidence is derived from the techniques being utilised. And those techniques need to be practiced. [Note: in the *Key Skills* part of this book there is a specific section on *decision making* which covers a process for making conscious 'thought-through' decisions which can then become unconscious and automatic. There is also an activity to carry out in order to embed this and a case study which illustrates a real example.]

In addition I would also suggest to Alan, or anyone wanting to work on this aspect of the Zone, that they read/practice other Key Skills such as problem solving, dealing with self limiting beliefs, developing intuition, and developing curiosity.

Alan looks at his watch and comments that this is the penultimate session. You understand this to mean that although the program's end is in sight, Alan realises his issues have not been fully resolved...

Tell Alan he is right, the program is coming towards its conclusion. As discussed early on, there is no pink ribbon that ties everything neatly together. There is no finish line. In the many hundreds of coaching experiences I have had, it is extremely unusual to have a neat end. It is very important that both the coach and Alan understand this. Of course, that is not an argument for leaving things untidy, at the end, but progress is a rolling process that does not just stop at the end of the eighth session.

It is beholden on both parties to be clear where they want to be at the end of the eighth session. Particularly Alan.

Remember that at session six Alan was tasked to revisit his skillset and rate where he thinks he is on a scale and to consider where he wants to be by the end of session eight? Now is the time to have that discussion with Alan - getting him to think through the skills he has developed already, how he can embed them, and how he can take them further. See the sample dialogue on dealing with this.

So, is the out-of-session task for Alan to continue examining and taking ownership of his development? In preparation for the final session?

Yes, I would continue that. I would ask Alan to come back to session eight with his thoughts about what he understood he needed to do, what he would require (which can be covered in session eight), and how (ultimately) to measure its effectiveness.

It is also obviously vital that Alan works on his decision making before session eight, plus other aspects of the Zone, so that he can be enabled to move on after the coaching has finished.

Sample Dialogue – Session Seven

This Sample Dialogue is part of the discussion regarding Alan's ranking task.

Coach: How did you get on with the ranking task we discussed last time?

Alan: When we discussed it last time I thought it would be easy, but I actually found it much harder than I expected.

Coach: Why do you think that was?

Alan: Well, firstly, I wasn't sure which skills to choose. Then I realised, as you suggested, that I should go back to the beginning and revisit the skills we first talked about. Then go through all the stuff we had covered and see what else had cropped up along the way.

Coach: And what did you find?

Alan: What was really weird was how much had changed.

Coach: In what way?

Alan: Well, some of the skills and issues I thought were really important at the beginning have either been sorted or actually gone away. I realised I was already quite good at them or, in reality, they weren't that important in the first place. Is that normal or is it just me not being very aware about myself?

Coach: I'm tempted to say: 'What do you think?' (laughs), but it's actually a really good point. In some ways it's one of my measures that the coaching process has been based on you and your skills and issues.

Alan: Why is that?

Coach: Now you are asking all the questions (laughs again). As we said at the beginning - although there is a shape and a structure to the coaching, it's not set in tablets of stone; it should be based on your requirements which inevitably will change and develop over the time we have worked together.

Alan: So it's not just me then?

Coach: Well it is you because your journey is yours, and unique, but - as we have said - it happens to everybody in their own way.

Now, you said you'd found it harder than you expected, let's be a bit more exact. Which specific skills were the hardest?

Alan: It was in relation to knowing when I am in the Zone. I'm okay with the prep, and reviewing it afterwards, but it's having the skill of knowing I am in the Zone.

Coach: Okay, let's go through some examples and see what we can find. Remember that one of the quirks of the Zone is that you may not know you are in it at the actual time; that's one of the reasons that the review is so important.

Just to complicate it even more, some people - if they realise they are in the Zone - may well come out of it because they are thinking consciously rather than trusting their processes and preparation. So give me a couple of examples for us to discuss so that we can establish how this works for you. We can then look forward and see how you can use this to move forward.

Session 7 – Case Study – Sport

This case study presents a different aspect of coaching for the Zone. The individual I had been working with (for some considerable time) was a cricketer who had achieved a large amount of success and, partly because of that, had been made captain of his club. This was something of a controversial decision, as rather like promoting the best salesman or accountant and hoping they will automatically be able to lead others, this individual had always taken care of himself and left others to do the same. A further complication was that he didn't really want to be captain but allowed himself to be persuaded by the coaches.

Previously, we had worked on an 'as needs' basis, when he felt he required support or assistance. This meant we met on a regular basis but rather than working on ongoing skills and issues we dealt with whatever was current for him. When the captaincy issue came along we were part-way through a process of re-jigging his processes in order to keep them fresh. At the seventh session he said he wanted to put his issues on the back burner and deal with becoming captain and, in particular, use his ability to get into the Zone to help the team.

The first point I made to him was that while it was possible for a team to get into the Zone, it presented different issues and that he might have to accept that the way that the team, and the individuals in it, wanted to do this, could differ from his own experiences. He struggled with accepting this so we decided that session seven would be a discussion between ourselves on the key issues plus some initial thoughts on how to move forward, bearing in mind his concern that he wanted to make an immediate impact.

As a product of this discussion the following key issues were identified and agreed:

- it was okay for individuals to develop or have their own ways of getting into the Zone
- however, there would be certain key processes that the whole team would need to commit to
- his way of doing things might be different, or not right for others
- equally, their ways might be better than his, for the team
- the coaches would also need to be involved

- not all the players or coaches would move forward at the same speed or with the same degree of commitment
- in the early stages it would not be helpful to get into a debate on measures of success; it would be better to make progress, and demonstrate success, before getting too hard headed.

In terms of specific actions we agreed that we needed to have a two hour working session with the players and coaches to discuss and agree how to move forward. In addition I would share some practical approaches to help individual players work on the Zone. As a consequence of this, if players wanted to work with me individually this would be supported by the captain and the club, but carried out under the umbrella of the team and its ability to get into the Zone.

Session 8

Final session. Alan comes in and thanks you. He says he understands that he is not the finished article. He will continue to use the techniques he has learned but wants to know what the next stage is.

Context would be very important here. Many companies, because they apply a budget to the programme would say 'that is it', and it would be up to Alan and the coach to discuss what might happen in the future.

Other organisations, particularly where the coach has an ongoing relationship with them, might say 'we want you to continue to have an informal relationship with Alan' so that the coachee feels they have access to the coach.

It is obviously important that we follow up on the work that Alan started through sessions six and seven. This would include revisiting: the ranking task to see if Alan had thought any more about this (plus had any more examples), his decision making and how he was going to move it forward, and what else he thought he needed to do (and how he was going to measure it).

It is also vital that time is given to the Zone and Alan's experiences of it. This should build on previous discussions and experiences and what Alan has learnt about his ability to get into the Zone more regularly. And how (if appropriate) he *intends* to be able to repeat his experiences of getting into the Zone.

As part of this, and depending on how well I thought Alan had achieved this, I might ask Alan if he had any examples of being in the Zone while going through the coaching process or even during the coaching sessions themselves. This may sound either obvious or inappropriate but sometimes coaches look at the skills they are working on as existing *outside* the coaching process (i.e. they don't see that coaching itself is an opportunity to experience/practice skills). Often this question gets the most amazing and important answers which can really change things for the coachee.

There are some weighty topics here and time should be allowed to cover them properly. However, the time should be managed as endless talking, reviewing, and analysing could actually damage the process and possibly put Alan off taking things forward. It's important that Alan is clear about what he intends to do and is looking forward to doing it and being responsible for achieving this.

Therefore the key areas to be addressed for both Alan *and the coach* involve a structured discussion around the following topics:

- what has gone on in the programme
- what has worked
- why has it worked
- how has it changed things
- what has not worked (which can be hugely insightful from a coaching/Zone perspective)
- why has it not worked
- where does that leave the coachee (and the coach)
- what are the measures/criteria for evaluating the success of the programme. These could be so-called 'soft' measures (i.e. personal opinion, feelings, observations etc.), or more organisational measures like appraisals, 360° feedback. See the section on this topic in the *Key Skills* part of this book.

The purpose of this discussion is to pull together what has gone on but more importantly to help Alan plan for the future. It should also include how Alan will feedback to the organisation (and in particular his Line Manager) so that his progress can be maintained and further developed.

This discussion should be led by Alan with the coach questioning and clarifying as needed. Two key points also need to be brought up in this discussion:

1. What has Alan (specifically) got coming up – from a work content point of view?

2.   What practice opportunities can Alan create outside work?

Thus, the key for Alan is that he does not feel abandoned, but feels equipped enough to try and carry things on, and is open to his own ongoing learning and development. Also that the integration of everything is as seamless for Alan, his Line Manager, and the Organisation as possible.

Other Key Points

As a part of this process it is also vital that the coach reviews and reflects on how the programme with Alan has gone from his own (practitioner's) point of view and what he/she can learn from, further develop, modify and change in order to improve his/her own effectiveness.

The coach should use the same or similar questions to those shown above which were used to help Alan clarify their own learning. I would normally do this within two weeks of the coaching finishing and revisit my thoughts again within three months to see how my thoughts had developed.

Based upon what comes out of this self-review the coach should then make plans for implementing identified changes with the organisation, plus any personal development actions.

Finally?

Thank Alan for the work he has put in over the period of the coaching and, if appropriate, encourage him to stay in touch and let you know how things are going.

Session 8 – Sample Dialogue

This sample dialogue is part of the discussion regarding how both Alan and the organisation want to integrate Alan's progress back into his normal job and how the coaching programme has gone. The discussion should be led by Alan prompted by the coach.

Coach: So, Alan, give me an overview of how the coaching has gone for you.

Alan: Overall I think it has gone really well. Sometimes I have struggled to see where I am going with it, and I am a bit bothered about what happens now it is finishing, but it has been a really interesting experience.

Coach: Okay, we can discuss all that. What specifically has worked for you?

Alan: There are a number of specifics. For example, I think I have improved my interpersonal skills and I am definitely a better time manager, but actually, although it is a bit more general, it's my confidence that has really improved.

Coach: In what way?

Alan: Well I just feel that I can handle pretty much anything that comes at me now.

Coach: Fine, give me couple of examples of where this has already happened.

Alan: Well there was the time when the MD bumped into me in the corridor and asked me to help him prepare for a big meeting he had coming up. Previously, I don't think he would have asked me and I would certainly have been like a rabbit in car headlights.

Coach: That's interesting, although you mentioned it at the time you didn't seem to place that much importance to it then.

Alan: That's true, I didn't realise its significance until later.

Coach: Let's talk about that in a bit more detail. Why do you think that was so significant?

Alan: [replies in a lot of detail]

Coach: Can you be more specific about what it demonstrates and how you think you can use it?

Alan: Because it shows I can work with, and impact on, senior management because they think I have something to offer.

Coach: How does that change things?

Alan: It means I can take that confidence into other aspects of my work and life.

Coach: Such as?

Alan: My dealings with other people and my abilities as a Manager.

Coach: Excellent, we will come back to this when we summarise at the end, so what didn't work for you in the coaching?

Alan: Well I did sometimes think that for every issue there was a different technique, and I didn't always feel that I had time to practice and integrate them.

Coach: That's a good point. Remember that although it may have felt like that, if you find something that works for you - I know you liked visualisation - you can use that technique across a wide variety of situations. All techniques are part of a menu. It's about choosing the right option for a situation that is really powerful. Anything else?

Alan: Not really. I notice you haven't mentioned the Zone yet although a lot of the coaching was about the Zone.

Coach: That's true. It's a tricky one to know when to bring it up. If we start with it the tendency is for it to dominate the discussion sometimes to the detriment of other skills... with issues being lost. So I now tend to let it find its own time to be discussed, and that is when you mention it. So tell me where you think you are with the Zone right now.

Alan: Well, I think the key thing for me now is that I understand how, at the time, you don't realise it's happening - and that can make it a bit off the wall and mysterious - actually there are a lot of practical things you can do to make it happen.

Coaching For The Zone

Coach: Such as?

Alan: You already mentioned visualisation. That's a big one for me.

Coach: What else?

Alan: Something I would never have thought of. Breathing and Centering. We only covered them in recent sessions but, used together, they are really powerful for me.

Coach: Anything else?

Alan: They are the big ones for me I think.

Coach: Overall where do you feel you are at with the Zone, and your development?

Alan: I think I have the necessary techniques to help me and I know where to go if I need anything else. But as I said at the beginning, it's the confidence that I have done it before so I can do it again that is the big point for me!

Session 8 – Case Study – Sport

This was unusual in that the biggest problem the coachee faced actually cropped up in the final session! Therefore, this case study deals with that issue as part of the last session.

In this case the individual was a rower who had achieved a lot of success, partly through their fitness but mainly through their mental toughness and their ability to never give in. The rower was an athlete who was capable of snatching victory from the jaws of defeat.

He had come to me because he recognised his ability to deliver when it counted but he had no idea how (i.e. "it just happened" or "something switched on"). He was also worried that if he worked out what he was doing, somehow he might lose it. An irrational fear, but not an unusual one.

Circumstance had forced his hand because, while we were working together, he had a dip in form and lost a couple of races he normally would have won. This had caused him to doubt himself, me, and the work we were doing together. Having spent a weekend pondering this he had decided to press on, tackle the issue, and see what happened.

In our previous sessions we had established that, for him, mental toughness and being able to switch it on, even if he did it unconsciously, was the same as being in the Zone. Also we had established that, for him, this meant a combination of creating empowering beliefs, a pre-play of appropriate visualisations, and using three or four affirmations.

What became apparent when we sat down to do a 'live' session (where he would do these processes with me watching him to observe and comment on what I saw) was that he was going through the motions and doing them automatically without evaluating their impact or whether they were actually achieving anything. When we went through what he had done (or not done!) when losing his two big races exactly the same thing happened (i.e. nothing).

At this point he wanted to scrap everything he had been doing and start again. My response was that this was certainly an option, however before doing that I thought we should re-work his current processes in order to freshen them up (but essentially leave them alone until tested once again in performance).

In the end this is what he decided to do and consequently not only did he regain his ability to deal with adversity and difficult situations he was able to get into the

Coaching For The Zone

Zone earlier in his performances, and also while training - the combination of which enabled him to achieve even greater success than before.

This was a classic situation where rather than leaping in and changing things too quickly it was essential to test the robustness and effectiveness of what had worked for him previously.

Key Skills

" *The chief function of the body is to carry the brain around* **"**

Thomas Edison

In this section we will examine which Key Skills can be used to help a Coach to get their coachees into the Zone on a more regular, consistent basis.

The importance of each of the skills will be explained and why they are specifically relevant to the Zone. The coach will be tasked to carry out at least one activity for each skill covered and example case studies will illustrate real-life examples of how each skill has been used. In addition example sample dialogues are used to show how each of the skills can be applied.

The purpose of these activities, case studies and sample dialogues is to help the coach see the importance of each of the skills covered and provide guidance on how to make best use of them. The coach should rigorously examine their own level of competence in each of the skills, and work on improving any which they believe require further improvement. In addition *Coaching For The Zone* can be used as a reference aide in-between sessions to review how the coaching is progressing and as a preparation tool for future sessions.

Because the Zone can be seen as something almost magical and mystical there can be a tendency to believe that the skills required to help people achieve it must also be the same. In fact the skills are the same ones used in all communication between people (e.g. husband and wife, people at work, doctor and patient, teacher and class).

Just because the skills are part of everyday life does not mean they should be taken for granted or that we should not understand their impact in helping people achieve their goal of getting into the Zone. In fact, the point that they are normal day-to-day skills means that we do not have to learn a whole set of new skills but make better use of the ones we already have.

So let's take a look at some of the Key Skills and how to make best use of them…

- creating rapport
- questioning
- giving and receiving feedback
- listening
- problem solving
- influencing
- decision making
- non-verbal communication
- dealing with emotions
- dealing with self-limiting beliefs
- intuition
- curiosity
- assisting learning
- using appropriate language patterns
- using metaphors and storytelling
- developing your own coaching style
- the impact of your own behaviour as a coach
- reviewing and learning from coaching for the Zone
- measuring and evaluating from coaching for the Zone

All of these skills are normal day-to-day skills which can be utilised by people in any walk of life. In other words it's not possible for human beings to communicate without using these skills. In turn, the effective use of these skills can have an enormous impact on the chances of any coach helping their coachee achieve the Zone state.

However, in coaching, as in many other contexts, these skills take on a particular emphasis which can massively help the coach achieve their goal of helping the coachee achieve their goal.

Creating Rapport

**QUOTE: Always forgive your enemies, nothing annoys them so much –
Oscar Wilde**

The topic of rapport is well established and recognised by most people. A
gathering of friends will comment on how well two (or more) of their circle seem
to be getting on. This is not an issue of scientific observation and if we were to
ask how they know, the response might be 'we just know'!

Yet normally there are many clues to rapport - some of which are matching,
mirroring, pacing and leading, and using appropriate language.

A greater awareness has developed into many of these activities since the advent
and increasing popularity of NLP. However, like many other aspects of NLP, all
that has really happened is that the implicit has become more explicit (a
worthwhile contribution in its own right, mind you).

In addition NLP has provided a number of activities that can help people practice
these skills. The use of these skills has led to accusations that NLP is being used
to manipulate people. It is not the purpose of this book to get involved in this
debate. However, as a number of the activities in this book have their origins in
NLP it is worth making the point that it all comes down to the intention of the
coach. It is vital (and normal) that the coach should have a *positive intent* for their
relationship with the coachee and their goals. Anything less than this will mean
that the relationship will be fractured and will not achieve effective results. In
other words it will not be possible to be effective without having and
demonstrating positive intent.

One key point to make here is that positive intent is not the same (necessarily) as
liking the person. This is a point that often causes confusion. There can be
obvious advantages in the coach liking the coachee (and vice versa). However,
this can also make the relationship too cosy and mean that real issues don't get
tackled or resolved. Personally I would aim for respect and trust in the
relationship and let 'being liked' take care of itself.

Creating Rapport – Activity

Whenever you are working with, or watching, people - consciously check to see if, in your opinion, they are in rapport. If you think people are in rapport it is highly likely that, to some extent, they are either in the Zone, or there is a stronger chance of them getting there. Then check to see what the evidence for this is. It's likely that you will find a combination of the following:

- smiling
- similar breathing patterns
- similar levels of eye contact
- similar non-verbal language (body language)
- similar posture
- similar gestures
- a pattern where one person does one of the above and the other follows shortly after (pacing and leading)
- similar pitch, pace, tonality in speech

If the coach is aware of the above (in themselves and their coachees) he or she can then, with a positive intent, use one or more of the above to demonstrate their rapport both with the individual as a person and, if appropriate, with what they are saying.

One other point is important regarding rapport. It is possible to deliberately break rapport by doing the opposite or something different to the coachee to show disagreement, without actually saying so in words.

Creating Rapport – Sample Dialogue

Coach: What skill - that you think you *don't have* - would you like to have?

MD: [Looks down, pauses, thinks deeply, then smiles] Well, this probably sounds stupid but I've always admired people with a good sense of humour.

Coach: In real life, or shows or characters on TV?

MD: Both. Of course in real life there needs to be a time and a place for it.

Coach: Maybe some people believe that humour is always appropriate. It depends on how it's done within a particular situation.

MD: I never thought of it like that although I went to a funeral recently where there was lots of humour and laughter and that was entirely in context with the guy who had died. He would have loved it.

Coach: So maybe that's the skill.

MD: Maybe. It would certainly make my meetings more fun.

Coach: Okay, you can pick up on that in a while. Who in particular do you find funny and why?

MD: [looking sheepish] Actually it's Monty Python.

Coach: It's often good to be surprised and you've just surprised me! What is it about Monty Python?

MD: Well, on one level it seems stupid and juvenile but on another level it's really clever and revealing.

Coach: In what way?

MD: It pricks the bubble of taking things over-seriously and being pompous.

Coach: So how could this help in your meetings?

MD: Not sure really, it's more of a feeling that it would lighten the mood, relax people, and make them more creative and responsive.

Coach: Okay, let's think of some ways we could give it a go.

Creating Rapport – Case Study

One skill not normally mentioned when creating rapport is using humour. As used to be the case in Reader's Digest's *Laughter Is The Best Medicine*. Recent studies have shown that this is true, even with life-changing illnesses. When two people, or a much larger group of people, are laughing or smiling there is either collective rapport or at least a basis for it.

Within coaching and as a way of creating the Zone humour is incredibly powerful.

One example of this was when dealing with an MD who seemed not to have a sense of humour; he appeared totally task driven. The sessions were normally very structured, focussed, and to the point. However, at one session he didn't seem to quite be himself. Normally, with him, I would just carry on and deal with the business at hand, but some instinct made me ask him to identify a skill that we hadn't discussed, and which he would like to work on. The sample dialogue (above) followed.

His response was amazing. He said he would like to be able to make people laugh while ensuring that they did their jobs. I asked him whose humour he admired and he mentioned Monty Python (which to me was even more amazing).

We then spent 10 minutes discussing what made Monty Python funny, revisiting some of their most famous sketches. The rapport between us at this point was outstanding and led to him realising that although the Monty Python type of humour might not always be appropriate, he could loosen up his style and still be just as effective (if not more so). In addition he would be creating rapport with his people which was one of the things he wanted to achieve.

For those people who are worried that using humour can be unprofessional or just plain wrong, or believe that they are simply not 'funny people', my answer is that it's *not* about telling jokes (or very rarely) it's about being able to read the situation and the people involved and with a deft turn of phrase move things forward in a purposeful way.

Creating Rapport – Case Study – Sport

One of the intriguing things about professional sport is that, in most sports, there can be a turnover each season of anything up to a third of the players (and sometimes the coaches and backroom staff). This can massively affect the team dynamic as players need to integrate very quickly so that personality issues don't adversely affect team morale and performance.

In this case study, a new player was joining a sports team. He had a strong track record regarding his performance but also a reputation for not being an easy person to deal with. This had been noted by the team's current players who waited for his arrival with mixed feelings.

One of the things we did as part of pre-season's team building was to run a session where the players told each other how they liked to be dealt with in the dressing room (e.g. when they had just performed badly or been told they had been dropped). This session was considered to be a fairly controversial way to build team spirit but we thought that the honesty it required would prove very beneficial.

One of the things that came out of the session was the way the so called 'difficult' player dealt with this. His eye contact virtually disappeared, his shoulders slumped, his breathing became quicker and more shallow, and as a consequence his complexion became blotchy. Also his language became more negative and his tone of voice became more clipped and harsh.

The other players, without being experts or trained in rapport, picked up on these signals and instead of backing off, or leaving him alone, started to ask him for more information about his reaction but without interrogating him or appearing as though they were trying to score points off him. The coaches also joined in - picking up the vibe from the players' approach.

The consequence of this was the player telling the story about being dropped by his national side but only finding out about it by hearing it on the radio as he was driving home from a trip out. Sharing this seemed to lift a weight from his shoulders and his posture and voice changed accordingly. He then visibly relaxed and joined in the rest of the session in a much more interactive way. This also positively impacted on the rest of the squad.

Questioning

QUOTE: It's not what you think you are that holds you back, it's what you think you are not – Unknown

Of all the coaching (and life) interpersonal skills there are, it is my observation that the ability to ask and respond to good quality questions is the most important. It is a skill that is either rarely practised, taken for granted, or used in an aggressive interrogative way. The right question(s) asked at the right time can create the 'aha' moment that is either the entry point to the Zone or confirmation, for the coach, that the coachee is actually in the Zone.

Key Skills

These Dos and Don'ts offer a framework for becoming effective at asking good quality questions. However, as one of my coachees said to me (a long while ago) "This list is obvious and simple to understand but it's probably the most difficult set of skills to actually do."

Questioning – Activity

Practice using the following checklist in order to 'Do the dos' and avoid the 'Don'ts'!

Do	*Don't*
Ask questions	Ask multiple questions
Ask one question at a time	Make statements
Ask open questions	Ask closed questions
Ask probing questions	Ask forced-choice questions
Stay open and neutral	Ask leading questions
Clarify	Jump to conclusions
Ask short to-the-point questions	Ask long, complicated questions
Be aware of non-verbals	Ignore non-verbals
Be prepared to listen	Switch off before they get to the real part

Again it's helpful to watch day-to-day interactions between people and look at the quality of that interaction and the results it achieves. You should expect to find that the higher the quality the more likely that good quality questions are a major factor.

Questioning – Case Study

An example of this was when I dealt with someone who was very unclear regarding what they wanted to get out of the coaching process. Through the Dos and Don'ts covered in this section it became clear that the real issue was committing to a course of action that might not work.

The skill here was to unpick and allow the coachee to find the real issue for themselves. This was achieved by simply using open questions: what, how, who, where, when, which (using, but avoiding too many whys); asking one question at a time and staying open and neutral.

In these situations it is also important to avoid the 'Don'ts' wherever possible. The three major faults are a) asking multiple questions b) asking leading questions and c) asking long complicated questions.

It should also be noted when looking at the 'Don'ts' list that they don't just occur on their own. In other words it's quite possible to ask questions using a combination of the 'Don'ts' (e.g. a long complicated, multiple, leading question that ends up as a forced choice!). Inevitably, in these circumstances, the questioner (not realising they have committed these errors) tends to blame the coachee for the poor quality of their response and any chance of getting in the Zone is gone.

Questioning – Sample Dialogue

This sample dialogue is based on part of the conversation with the coachee covered in the Case Study.

Coach: What would you like to work on as part of coaching for the Zone?

Coachee: I'm not really sure, have you got any thoughts or ideas that might help me?

Coach: The real skill with this is identifying things regarding the Zone that are directly relevant to you. What are some of the key things you've got coming up where the Zone will be relevant?

Coachee: Well. there are lots of things coming up here at work.

Coach: Such as?

Coachee: The company is restructuring which is bound to impact on me and my team.

Coach: Anything else?

Coachee: That's the big one but I'm not sure what I can do about it at this point or how the Zone might help me.

Coach: Why is that?

Coachee: I'm not sure how helpful the Zone could be in this situation.

Coach: Because?

Coachee: It seems to be a bit too self-indulgent and too much about me!

Coach: Why do you think that?

Coachee: Isn't the Zone just about me trying to feel good about myself?

Coach: That may be part of it. What would be the benefits to you, your team, and the company if you chose to work on the Zone?

Coachee: I'm not sure… can I have some time to think about it?

Coach: Sure. What would be the things you would want to think about?

Coachee: Well I wouldn't want to work on anything that might not work.

Coach: Why is that?

Coachee: It would be a waste of time and embarrassing.

Coach: Which of those is the most serious?

Coachee: I don't want to be embarrassed by being seen to do something that hasn't worked.

Coach: Has this happened before?

Coachee: Not really, although we have gone through a lot of changes together.

Coach: So?

Coachee: So, the company is used to me trying out new things.

Coach: Has everything always worked in the past?

Coachee: (laughs) No. Of course not.

Coach: So what's the real issue here?

Coachee: I guess I don't want to look and feel a failure if the Zone stuff doesn't work.

Coach: How can we use this concern to enable you to move forward?

Coachee: I think I need to commit to it, and give it everything, and be open with everyone about what I am doing.

Coach: Okay, where should we start?

Questioning – Case Study – Sport

This scenario involved a professional cricketer who had been told that his contract would not be renewed for the following season. As far as he was concerned this came completely "out of the blue" and was wrong and unfair. His reaction was that he wanted to stay and fight for his place while the club was happy to let him go immediately, or as soon as suited him.

The player felt that he hadn't been properly managed nor kept in the picture regarding what was expected of him, something the club and coaches did not accept as they had procedures in place to deal with these issues (including regular reviews).

As frequently happens in these circumstances the 'truth' was a matter of judgement and opinion and reactions were based more on emotion than substance. I had worked with the player on an occasional basis, so he asked to talk things through with me.

The first thing that became apparent was that the heat and emotion he felt were making it difficult for him to move forward and plan for his future. He still felt that if he could stay, fight, and perform well for the rest of the season - that would solve the problem.

My thoughts in preparing for the meeting were that we would need to start with what had occurred and allow him to vent his feelings before moving onto his thoughts and plans for the future. Therefore I planned to ask lots of open questions, listen intently, and by doing this (and without being judgemental) allow him to see that - in fact - he hadn't actually performed to the required standard (before looking at the future).

What actually happened was, to my surprise, that he didn't want to rehash the current situation. He felt that he had more than enough people around him to do this, so he wanted to use the session to brainstorm some ideas regarding his options and ideas for his future.

Therefore the point of the questioning skills, and how best to use them, was not to have pre-planned questions lined up to just be rolled out, with the intention of helping, but to treat them like a menu and have the skill and flexibility to do the 'Do's' and avoid the 'Don'ts' (i.e. ask open questions, avoid multiple, leading and closed questions, probe further when appropriate, in order to make the session helpful to the individual).

Giving and Receiving Feedback

It is totally deliberate that both the giving and receiving of feedback are mentioned in this section. Some coaches operate on the basis that their role is only to provide feedback and it is not appropriate for them to receive any. This is absolutely incorrect and will severely limit the chances of the coachee (or the coach) getting into the Zone.

One other point to clarify is the difference between feedback and criticism (even if it is labelled as 'constructive').

Some basic principles regarding the differences are:

- criticism focuses on the person, whereas feedback focuses on the behaviour or situation
- criticism is general and feedback is specific
- criticism is evaluative, blaming and fault finding, while feedback is remedy seeking
- criticism dwells on what happened, the past; feedback emphasises what will be done, the future
- criticism is often saved up, feedback is timely.

Specifically this means that effective feedback:

- describes the behaviour
- is direct
- is genuinely meant by the sender
- is checked for clarity
- utilises relevant questions
- has specific consequences
- refers to behaviours which are under the receiver's control
- affirms the receiver's positive intent
- affirms the relationship

Whereas ineffective feedback:

- evaluates and judges the behaviour
- is delayed and saved up
- transfers ownership
- denies feelings
- is general, indirect or vague
- is not checked for clarity
- is irrelevant
- asks poor quality questions
- refers to behaviours which are not under the receiver's control
- is distorted by the sender's needs
- denies the receiver's positive intent.

There is a lot of needless debate regarding the effectiveness (or otherwise) of negative and positive feedback and in psychology there are lots of studies regarding negative and positive reinforcement.

Although most coaches would accept that positive feedback is more likely to be useful, some worry themselves about being false, condescending, or patronising.

The key point about both forms of feedback is that they should be real and specific (i.e. there is no point in making up something just to create a topic to provide feedback on, and definitely don't overpraise a coachee by going 'over the top' regarding a perfectly normal skill or response).

Giving and Receiving Feedback – Activity

Some guidelines to help the coach get this balance right are:

Negative Feedback:

- express your concern/observation in specific terms
- ensure you understand/or ask for the whole story or context
- use the appropriate skills of feedback covered in this section (e.g. listening, questions, etc.)
- clarify the reasons for the incident
- reinforce any correct performance
- discuss alternatives
- agree future courses of action with coachee.

Positive Feedback:

- Use 'I' statements to describe your reactions. Avoid 'you', 'we', 'us', 'everybody', 'nobody'
- Base the feedback on a specific behaviour or situation (e.g. "The question you used to clarify the situation changed things" not "You obviously jumped in without thinking")
- Focus on the needs of the coachee. Don't drift into your own skills, thoughts, or issues
- Give feedback only when it can effect change. Even with positive feedback there is a wrong time to give it (as many parents learn to their cost). Therefore only provide feedback when it can effect change and/or development.
- Avoid giving mixed messages. Focus on the specific skill or situation.
- Avoid lapsing into pseudo-investigation. Be careful of overusing 'why'. If you find the coachee over-explaining or becoming defensive about their behaviour, even though your feedback is intended to be positive, you have drifted into other territory.
- Avoid overload – no matter how well intentioned the weakest item in your feedback will be the one the coachee focuses on at the expense of the point you were really trying to make.
- Let the coachee decide a) what they think of the feedback and b) what future action they will take.

Giving and Receiving Feedback – Case Study

This case study involves dealing with someone who, through playing sport to a high standard, knew about and understood the Zone. However, he had not initially thought about it in the context of work but then realised he had been in the Zone at work and so had his team.

The key to this example was getting the coachee involved in his company's 360° feedback process. To his total surprise the coachee received a lot of negative feedback, particularly regarding his interpersonal skills. Initially he was negative and hostile to the feedback but when, through the coaching, he realised that in his sports he only played individual sports (i.e. golf, skiing, running marathons) - the penny dropped. This led to him admitting that he had always avoided being coached in his sports because he didn't want to be told what he was doing wrong.

This then provided a platform for him to take the following steps.

 a) Share his feedback with his team (which he wasn't obliged to do)
 b) Be open about his reaction to it
 c) Within the session he ran with his team plan to avoid his tendency to avoid, blame, justify, condone, excuse, deny or justify his own actions
 d) Explain about his love of sports and his interest in the Zone and how he would like to work on them both individually and with the team
 e) Ask for suggestions as to how he could tackle these issues and move forward
 f) Commit to a plan of action which he would review regularly with his team
 g) Revisit the 360° feedback process again in 12 months

One other outcome was that he, and the team, decided to organise a Zone Day within which a combination of fun and serious work tasks would be used. I was invited to design and facilitate this session which was then used as a platform for their ongoing work programmes.

Giving and Receiving Feedback – Sample Dialogue

This sample dialogue is based on part of the discussion in the Case Study regarding the coachee's reaction to their 360 feedback.

Key Skills

Coach: What is your first reaction to the 360 feedback?

Coachee: To be honest I'm not sure how accurate or relevant it is.

Coach: Why is that?

Coachee: Well, I don't think it's right.

Coach: In what way?

Coachee: Mainly because I don't recognise myself in the feedback.

Coach: In what way specifically?

Coachee: I come across as arrogant and abrupt and not really interested in helping my people.

Coach: Go on.

Coachee: It just doesn't seem fair.

Coach: So what is the key issue here? Is it the accuracy of the feedback, its relevance, or the fairness?

Coachee: Ah, I see your point. You think I'm reacting this way because I don't like the feedback.

Coach: That can happen sometimes but it's really about helping us to agree on your reaction then deciding on actions to move forward.

Coachee: Do you think it's accurate?

Coach: That's not really the point is it?

Coachee: No, I know that, but it would be interesting to know.

Coach: Maybe, but would it help you move forward?

Coachee: I'm not sure.

Coach: Okay, so how should we move forward?

Coachee: I suppose I should try and work through the 360 and try and pin down some specifics.

Coach: Good idea. Remember to look for strengths as well… so that we can further develop these and not just take them for granted.

Coachee: Good point, I'd forgotten all about the good stuff.

Giving and Receiving Feedback – Case Study 2

This Case Study builds on the Case Study already covered in this section, and deals with the part of the conversation regarding the coachee's sport.

The key part of this was the coachee realising that all the sports he had played, and his experiences of being in the Zone, were based on him as an individual, something he hadn't realised before.

This emerged through a discussion during the coaching session into how he had achieved the Zone, and how he had worked on improving his levels of performance. I asked him about what feedback he had received and how he had responded to it. His answer was that he hadn't really received any; he had worked things out for himself. We then discussed how helpful the small amounts of feedback had been and his view was that, most of the time, it had been fine.

My suggestion at this point was to say I thought we should break the discussion down into those two areas (i.e. when feedback had been fine, and also when it hadn't). He thought this was okay and suggested we start with when it had been fine. He then went on to describe a number of situations when he had had to overcome difficult situations in his various sports and how he had done so.

I pointed out that all the situations he had described were negative. At this point he looked puzzled and said that obviously they were - as that's what feedback was for. I asked the coachee what he thought the differences were between self-criticism and feedback and his view was that they were pretty much the same thing. I then shared with him some of the principles of positive and negative feedback and the differences between them. We also discussed how best to give and receive feedback either to (and with) others, or just by oneself.

The coachee then pointed out that when he analysed the times when his approach hadn't worked he had pretty much failed to adhere to any of the principles of effective feedback and that often - when it had worked - it was only because it forced him to deal with something. Not because he wanted to, but because he thought he should.

We then went on to discuss what impact this had had on his mood, morale, and motivation regarding his sports, what lessons he could learn from this, and what he could do for his team at work based on these lessons.

Listening

QUOTE: The key to being the best is to train your mind and emotions equally as well as you train your body – Unknown

The topic of listening seems so obvious that it can feel embarrassing to mention it ... and yet it always (quite rightly) does require mentioning.

With listening, there is a distinction between 'being quiet but waiting for an opportunity to speak' and actually 'actively' listening to what is being said. Where this latter action becomes relevant is when the coach (who is listening) detects nuances and subtleties regarding 'how' something is being said, or what is 'not' being said. This enables them to get a fuller picture and almost certainly leads them to ask further questions which then allow the coachee to clarify their own thinking.

One of the oldest maxims that many people remember being told when they were young is that we were given two ears and one mouth and that they should be used in that proportion!

This can be extremely difficult for the coach who thinks their role is to 'tell' the coachee the correct answers rather than ask questions and then truly listen to the coachee's responses.

On a wider front, nearly every negative interaction between people is, at some point, described by one party as 'you know what their problem is? They never listen'. If someone finds themselves having to tell someone else that they were listening, it's too late, the die is already cast.

Some guide points for the coach who wants to work on their listening skills are:

The Coach:

- is highly aware of the coachee's non-verbal communication
- is listening to what is being said in the 'here and now' not drifting into analysing the past or predicting the future
- has good rapport
- is comfortable with the coachee being open, and able to open themselves up, if appropriate
- is relaxed, poised, focused, and confident
- is able to encourage further clarification of key issues
- allows the coachee to find their own answers
- is not distracted by their own prejudices and preferences about people, or the 'correct answers'
- is able to withhold judgement until they are sure they have the full story
- is able to paraphrase, reflect, integrate, summarise and challenge the coachee appropriately

Research suggests that the brain processes information at least four times faster than the speed of the spoken word. The only problem with this is that it allows the mind of the listener to drift into other areas while still either pretending to listen or, worse, actually believing they are listening.

For the coachee to get into the Zone there is more chance of this occurring while they are actually talking (and being listened to) than when the coach is talking all over them.

This is particularly true if the coach is handling the situation by using the skills covered in this section on interpersonal skills and the criteria for this is using the ones appropriate to both the coachee and the situation.

Listening – Activity

Practice the following listening skills both within and outside the coaching situation:

- try saying "So if I hear you correctly..." and reflect back what has been said. If there is any element of interpretation, assumption, or judgement, label it as such but if possible avoid it altogether.

Key Skills

- try this four stage process to see how well you do –

  a) listen very carefully to what the coachee is saying
  b) identify the coachee's key experiences: what they say is happening to them
  c) identify the coachee's key behaviours: what they are doing, not doing, or trying to do
  d) identify the key feelings and emotions associated with these experiences and behaviours

The key to being an effective listener is being able to totally focus on the listener while, at the same time, suspending judgement on either them, or what they are saying.

Listening – Case Study

One of the issues regarding listening, which sounds counterintuitive, is an overemphasis on the content at the expense of how the words are said.

An example of this was when I was dealing with a highly successful, female, media executive. She was an extremely strong, forceful personality who didn't brook disagreement and operated at an incredibly fast rate of work. Because of her role and seniority she assumed that people genuinely always thought she was right and felt good about doing what she wanted. She agreed to the coaching in order to further develop her career and because she realised that recently, for reasons she didn't understand, her style seemed not to be working as effectively.

The point about listening was established when she invited me to sit in on an important presentation she was giving and then do a one-to-one debrief with her afterwards.

During the presentation it was obvious that, although she noted the words being used in the questions she completely missed many of the nuances, underlying issues, or real feelings people had.

During the presentation I noted the question being asked but also what seemed to be the real question, issue, point. Afterwards, during the debrief, she defended herself by saying, "I answered the questions they asked me." When probed as to whether she had achieved her goal of getting full commitment and a yes decision she said she knew she hadn't.

As an outcome to the debrief my coachee volunteered to prepare a review of her presentation, her answers to the questions asked, and then comment on what she considered to be the real, underlying issues and concerns, and comment on each of these as a way of moving forward. She then did a follow-up presentation where she involved and engaged with the team more and listened and responded to what the team was really saying.

At no stage had we referred to the Zone in any of our sessions but shortly afterwards, while a group of us were having coffee, someone I had been working on the Zone with mentioned it in passing. After the coffee my media executive client asked me about the Zone and said that she'd never heard about it before but it fitted with how she had felt while running the second more open presentation session.

Listening – Case Study – Sport

This case study illustrates the point that listening is hard work for many people, which is one reason why many people either can't do it, or can't be bothered to do it.

The background was a professional football club where the manager had been a very successful international player who, after retiring, had gone into management at the highest level and initially done well. However, as his career developed, he seemed to lose his way and his team's performances started to suffer. This culminated in him leaving the club and having time out of management. After a period of time he became the manager of a club two leagues below where he had managed previously.

I contacted him to see if he would let me interview him for a book on Sport Psychology I was working on at that time. He very kindly agreed and I arranged to meet him to do the interview. On the day of the appointment I travelled to his new club - excited to go through my interview and to meet a legend of the game.

One of the questions I asked him was: what was the biggest learning point for him in making the transition from the top of the Premier League to a club somewhat below that level. At this point he smiled ruefully and told me a story about his first day in the job.

Key Skills

He had turned up at the training ground to watch the team training and had been surprised and disappointed by the low level of skill he saw. Finally he was unable to contain himself and he went onto the pitch and told the players what he thought. The players responded by going quiet and avoiding eye contact with him. His subsequent response was to grab one of the practice balls and demonstrate what he wanted them to do.

This was greeted by continued silence from the players, finally broken by one player saying: "It's okay for you to be able to do it, Boss, but we can't. And you've made us feel small and stupid." At this point the manager realised the player was right; he had demonstrated no interest in them as people and players, or recognised anything regarding their current levels of skill and application. Without meaning to - he had created a barrier between them and himself.

He immediately realised the potential damage he had caused by not listening to his players first and finding out more about them before stepping in. He described this to me as the biggest lesson he had learnt as a manager.

Problem Solving

QUOTE: There is nothing so useless as doing efficiently that which should not be done at all – Peter Drucker

Probably the greatest debate in coaching is to what extent the coach should solve the coachee's problem(s). The responses to this range from a) not at all because the coachee has all the resources they need, they just need help to find them to b) do whatever is necessary even if it means instructing the coachee directly.

Regarding the Zone it is my experience that a) works better than b) both in terms of consistency and getting into the Zone, but that, occasionally b) can provide the key breakthrough, provided it is based on the coachee's own actions.

Inevitably the start point is establishing what the *real* problem is rather than the *perceived* problem. In regard to the Zone it is astonishing how often the key breakthrough is the coachee realising that a) it's not really a problem at all or b) it's a different problem to the one they thought it was and normally this means it is easier to resolve.

Problem Solving Activity

A well-known problem solving framework is as follows:

- with the coachee, explore the current situation
- define the specific issue
- review all the possible options
- filter these based on the coachee's values, attitudes, and beliefs
- explore the coachee's hunches, intuition, and best guesses about what will work
- prioritise the various options available
- think through the various alternatives, risks, and consequences of the priorities
- ask the coachee what their first steps/actions will be
- agree the various blocks to these steps/actions
- brainstorm/find solutions to these blocks or at least those with the best chance of success
- agree an action plan
- regularly review and update the action plan

At some point, if this process is working effectively there will a breakthrough; a different perspective, a shift in thinking, a more positive attitude to taking action. The coach's role at this point is to 'act as co-pilot but not to fly the plane'.

Problem Solving – Case Study – Sport

It is likely that at the heart of all coaching, and in particular coaching for the Zone, that a problem will exist.

The problem of course might be a positive one (e.g. how to get into the Zone, how to stay in the Zone, how to get into the Zone on a more regular basis). The key is to be, on one hand, absolutely clear in identifying the problem but, at the same time, aware and observant enough to recognise how and when the problem changes and evolves.

This was brought home when coaching a sportsperson who was on the edge of establishing himself in a professional rugby team. At this point his performances slipped and the likelihood of his dream and objective was threatened. No-one could work out what had happened so I was asked to do a couple of coaching sessions with the player.

At the first session the player re-stated his objective of getting in, then staying in, the first team. He also had lots of experiences of the Zone and was very clear about how it had helped him. Then, after a pause, he said that it hadn't happened recently "thank goodness".

The 'thank goodness' was obviously a surprise and I realised he hadn't realised he had said it, so I asked him what the implications of getting into the Zone on a regular basis were, and therefore what becoming a First Team player meant. He paused and then said, "It means people will expect me to perform at a higher level on a consistent basis." This is a very common experience in the management world in general.

Therefore the real problem to be solved for him was not getting into the Zone and the First Team but dealing with the higher expectations of coaches, teammates, supporters, friends, family, and the general public. So without realising it, he had been self-sabotaging. Once this was highlighted he was able to move on to achieve his original objective.

Problem Solving – Case Study

This case study is a fairly typical one in virtually all management situations. However, although this example happened in a sporting situation it is included as a normal case study because of its wider application.

One of the interesting things about sport is that it is not played all year round but in seasons. Therefore there is time when the players and coaches are away from the club, and a time when they return in order to prepare for the next season. Even though there may have been a turnover of players, the majority will be the same. This means most of them will have been through many pre-season team building events previously, and are probably cynical about them and what they can actually achieve.

In discussing and planning a pre-season with some coaches I realised there was a danger of actually embedding a lot of negative feelings at the beginning of the season - obviously the opposite of what was intended! At this point I suggested we should consider doing something regarding the Zone. The coaches thought this was a good idea but were concerned about how we put it across to the players.

My response was that we should consider running an open session on the Zone and get the players to discuss and share their experiences rather than formally lecturing them on something that had to be experienced. The coaches' initial concern was that the players might think we were ducking the problem of running an effective pre-season session and dumping it on them. I pointed out that, in fact, what we were discussing was (in many ways) a more difficult way of tackling the problem. If we involved the players, properly, not only would we have solved the pre-season problem but we would have set up a potentially powerful process in order to help them.

Problem Solving – Sample Dialogue

Coachee: As you know I've had a lot of experience of the Zone, but not recently thank goodness.

Coach: (surprised) Why do you say thank goodness?

Coachee: Did I really say that?

Coach: Yes, any reasons why?

Coachee: (thinks and pauses) Well I suppose it has relieved the pressure a bit.

Coach: What pressure?

Coachee: The pressure to perform and keep performing to a high standard.

Coach: Did it feel like pressure when you were in the Zone?

Coachee: No, quite the opposite. The pressure comes separately to the Zone and sometimes it's difficult to handle.

Coach: In what way?

Coachee: There's never any escape from it. Everyone around you, even family and friends have an incredibly high level of expectation… but the worst part is the internal pressure.

Coach: Which is?

Coachee: The pressure I put on myself.

Coach: Has this been getting worse recently then?

Coachee: Yes and it has affected my form.

Coach: And has this impacted on your ability and willingness to get into the Zone?

Coachee: It must have yes.

Coach: So the real problem here is what?

Coachee: (thinks) The real problem is I am avoiding getting into the Zone, not because I can't, but because when I am in the Zone it's fine, but once I am outside the Zone I am putting extra pressure on myself.

Coach: Okay, so how do we carry on using the Zone and use it to help you to manage the pressure better ?

Coachee: I hadn't thought about using the Zone to help me deal with the pressure. Let me have a think about it.

Influence

QUOTE: Those who agree with us may not be right but we admire their astuteness – Unknown

In some ways this should be called positive influencing as it is, of course, quite possible to influence negatively. However, as this book is about coaching and the Zone it is within the spirit of these topics to focus on positive influencing.

Under Influence in *Longmans Synonym Dictionary* are words such as: affect, sway, bias, incline, change, alter, modify, act on, play on, transform, impress, impact upon, effect, move, impel, motivate, actuate, incite, arouse, instigate, induce, persuade – not a bad list for a coach helping someone achieve the Zone.

The classic model of influence breaks it down into these five key styles – persuading, asserting, bridging, attracting, and moving away - all of which can be useful and relevant. Persuading and asserting are described as *push* styles (i.e. the direction and energy is from Person A who is trying to influence, to Person B the recipient). Bridging and attracting are described as *pull* styles (i.e. although Person A is still the influencer they are using skills that gets Person B to make the movement).

Within this model moving away is viewed as a tactic which is neutral and used to change the energy, unblock a situation, and then to go back to push or pull.

In persuading there are two key behaviours:

- proposing and reasoning

In asserting there are three key behaviours:

- stating expectations, evaluating, using incentives and pressures

In bridging there are three key behaviours:

- involving, listening, disclosing

In attracting there are two key behaviours:

- finding common ground, visioning

In moving away there are two key behaviours:

- disengaging, avoiding

In the context of coaching it's easy to think that although all of the above are equally valid (provided they are used appropriately) it is more likely that it will be the pull styles (i.e. bridge and attract) that will be dominant and this is obviously likely. However, persuade and assert also have a large role to play.

For the purposes of this book it is not the intention to go deeper into the model, rather to point out its existence. The key thing is being flexible enough to use the appropriate approach, defined by the individual, the situation, the objectives, and style in order to be effective rather than roll the one we like best or use the most.

Key Skills

Some key factors that help in this choice are:

- make dialogue two-way – in fact the evidence would suggest that the balance of dialogue (i.e. who speaks the most) should be approximately 2/3 coachee and 1/3 coach
- use questions to uncover information, ideas, ways forward, objections
- help the coachee visualise what any suggestions mean to them
- focus on observable behaviour – be specific if you move into conjecture or assumptions, label your own behaviour (i.e. make it clear that you are doing so)
- probe to get beneath the surface in order to get to values, attitudes, beliefs and identity; particularly when these are likely to be the springboard for ongoing change.

In summary a useful set of steps to help achieve positive influence is:

1. Help the coachee identify what they 'need and want'
2. Help them to create a range of possibilities
3. Clarify and agree specific outcomes based upon "In light of Steps 1 and 2 what do I really want"
4. Clarify and agree "What am I willing to do (positively) in order to achieve the outcomes?"
5. What are the benefits and costs of these actions?
6. How will I measure my success?

Influence – Activity

The activity for this interpersonal skill is an unusual one. It is to carry out the steps listed above being aware of the key factors mentioned. In addition to read the best book I have read on the subject which is *Influence – Science & Practice* by Robert B. Cialdini. This book has been around for many years and is still relevant and up-to-date.

Influence – Case Study

This case study is based upon the influence model covered in the main section. My natural preference, as a coach, is for the pull style (i.e. bridge and attract). This is not a conscious preference, it's one that I feel comes naturally.

However, when dealing in the corporate world with highly committed, motivated people it can be very important to use the push style (i.e. persuade and assert).

This particular example involved a senior manager who was very concerned about respect. To some extent it was old fashioned respect (title and status rather than performance). It was important to recognise how important this was to him and while not really approving of it, be flexible enough to respond appropriately.

Another relevant factor was that my coachee had been told to go through a coaching programme rather than volunteering for himself.

At the first session he was direct - to the point of rudeness - and it became apparent that the session was going nowhere. I tried some of the pull style behaviours which he rode right over so I deliberately moved to assert myself to make my point and explain the benefits of coaching then moved to persuade him so that he could see how coaching would benefit him in his job and career.

At a subsequent session, and because influence was an important factor in his job, I explained the model to him emphasising how it required flexibility and skill and the ability to be able to read both people and the situation and he agreed to work on the bridge and attract behaviours as he realised he tended not to use them.

Influence – Case Study – Sport

This case study is related to a session with an athlete who was a high achiever and nationally ranked but seemed to choke on the really big occasions (something she was in denial about, and blamed on other circumstances; e.g. the weather, the track, etc.). We had discussed the Zone but, while expressing an interest, she had avoided doing anything about it. In preparing for the session I decided that, if required, I would use the Zone as part of helping her commit to something positive to help her move forward.

The opportunity arose in the session when she said that everything was too difficult and hard and that no matter what she did something always went wrong.

Key Skills

At this point I decided to use the six questions covered in the main body of this section but modified them for the Zone and her commitment to it.

To question 1 "What did she need and want from the Zone ?" - she replied that she wanted to be consistently able to finish her competitions on a high, knowing she had given her all.

To question 2 "What ways of achieving had she thought of?" - she initially struggled then narrowed matters down to retaining her focus and believing in herself.

Regarding the outcomes part of question 3 she wanted to achieve more top three finishes and improve her national ranking to be in the top four.

The really powerful question, which brought about the biggest change, was number 4 - regarding what she would do 'positively' to make it happen. This seemed to open the floodgates and she came up with a number of actions, the main one being a total mental and physical commitment to the Zone. She was then able to develop a list of the benefits and costs required to achieve that commitment.

The measures of success were as defined in question 4, plus performance measures built into her training and mental practice.

This 6 step process then allowed us to develop a workable plan to help her achieve the Zone and therefore improve her performances.

Influence – Sample Dialogue

This sample dialogue is based on part of the discussion with the senior manager mentioned in the general case study.

Coachee: I can't see any point in this. It's just a charade.

Coach: In what way?

Coachee: It just is.

Coach: How does that make you feel?

Coachee: Pissed off and annoyed.

Coach: What would be a more purposeful way to respond?

Coachee: I'm not interested in being more purposeful.

Coach: What are you interested in?

Coachee: Not this. You are just playing games and it's not very helpful.

Coach: What's the best thing I can do to help?

Coachee: Cut the crap and tell me straight.

Coach: Okay, what do you want to know?

Coachee: What is the point of this coaching?

Coach: Is it enough that the company says so?

Coachee: (laughs) Good one. Yes it probably is.

Coach: Remember that although you didn't choose me, I didn't choose you either.

Coachee: Fair point, so where does that leave us?

Coach: The company are into this so we can use it to move you forward and further develop your career.

Coachee: Sure, but it all feels a bit namby pamby.

Coach: Okay then, let's agree some rules for working together and we can make them as robust as you want.

Coachee: What do you mean?

Coach: Let's agree not just goals for you, but how open and robust we will be with each other.

Coachee: We can do that can we?

Coach: We sure can. Let's give it a go.

Decision Making

**QUOTE: The only thing that interferes with my learning is my education –
Albert Einstein**

With decision making a key area is not just who is making the decisions, but 'on
whose behalf?' too.

Normally in a coaching situation and particularly when it comes to the Zone it's
not possible (or right) for the coach to make decisions on behalf of the coachee.
For any fundamental change or development to take place it needs to be coachee-
driven. However this doesn't mean that the coach is not making any decisions.
Every situation they are in requires a combination of decisions: some pragmatic,
some logical, some intuitive. The ability to think on one's feet as well as plan
ahead is vital for one to become an effective coach.

One twist with decision making is that the coach is often looking to help the
coachee improve *their* decision-making skills. Many coachees struggle with
decision making particularly when connected to their own personal development.
They may be able to make decisions regarding spending large amounts of money,
or the purchase of a piece of equipment, but often they struggle with decisions
about people, particularly themselves.

When it comes to the Zone, other than in the planning stages, it's not possible to
consciously decide 'now I am going to enter the Zone'. Good conscious decision
making will help but it will be the unconscious, on the spur of the moment,
decisions that will make all the difference.

For the conscious process, thought-through structural decisions work very well.
For other decisions read the section on Intuition.

1. Identify – exactly what the problem is
2. Decide – how to solve it including brainstorming and evaluation
3. Action – plan it, do it
4. Review – what worked, what didn't, what can be learnt

Inevitably reducing a complex process to these simple steps runs the risk of
trivialising it. However the problem that many coachees have with decisions is

that they a) either jump in too quickly or b) tackle the wrong problem and therefore make the wrong decision.

To put a little more flesh on the bones here are some sub-steps for each of the above.

Decision Making – Activity – Choose a Decision that Needs to be Made

1. Identify – the kind of decision needs to be made; e.g. people, money, technical.

   - Why is the decision required now?

   - What are the benefits in making the decision?

   - What are the consequences of not making a decision?

   - How big is the problem?

   - How often does the problem occur?

   - When did the problem start and why?

2. Decide - do I need a 'one shot' final solution or will a short term solution be okay?

   - How much time and money do I have available?

   - What will be the effect on other people?

   - What will be my success criteria for the decision?

   - How do I rank those criteria in order of importance?

   - Regarding solutions can I:

        - see the problem from a different perspective?

- redefine the issue?

- remove some constraints?

- seek assistance from other people?

- use brainstorming or other techniques?

- what are the benefits/implications for each potential solution?

- would any of the solutions create further problems?

3. Action - who do I need to involve in implementing the decision?

    - How do I need to communicate the decision?

    - Will anyone need retraining?

    - Could there be any resistance, if so how will I overcome it?

    - How will I monitor the implementation of the decision?

4. Review - review against the acceptability criteria you have established.

    - Looking from now – what are potential successes and failures of the decision?

    - Projecting ahead – imagine what the potential successes and difficulties are.

    - Be as logical as possible – but don't over-analyse.

    - Decide who to implement and how.

Decision Making – Case Study

This situation involved someone who preferred to respond to things as they occurred; someone who preferred to be spontaneous and 'fly by the seat of their pants'. In the early stages of their career this had served them well and people enjoyed the more 'maverick' element of their approach.

As their career progressed and they started to take on greater responsibility, both people and financial, this approach didn't serve them so well, so coaching was suggested as a way of helping.

The individual knew about the Zone and liked the concept because of its random nature, so was surprised when I pointed out how much planning, pre-work, and decision making went into preparing to get into the Zone. Intrigued by this my coachee asked me how I would approach a specific issue she was facing at the time regarding someone she might promote.

Her argument was that people decisions had to be made through intuition as being natural and logical wouldn't work. Together we worked on the process laid out earlier and modified it to suit her current situation, something which appealed to her more creative side. We then used it to help her come to a decision.

Decision Making – Case Study – Sport

This involved an extremely successful sportsman who had achieved virtually everything possible within his sport. He had always said that he would know the moment to go but, now that the moment was approaching, he was struggling to make the decision.

During one of our sessions he mentioned this and said that he found it confusing and demoralising. We discussed this for a while and I asked him if there was anything in his sporting experiences that he thought might help him. He said he didn't understand the question but that he was willing to try anything. I pointed out to him that his great performances had involved being in the Zone so why not try the approaches he had used (to get into the Zone in his sport) for his decision about when to retire. He was intrigued by this but not sure how to go about it.

After a discussion we decided that he would go through the mental preparation routines he had developed for his sport and as part of this I would use the I – Identify, D – Decide, A – Action. R – Review process covered in the main body of this section on him by asking him the relevant questions from each of the four stages, in other words combine the best practice examples he had already developed and trusted with a more structured approach which he felt was required for his decision about retirement.

We did this and this enabled him to make a decision he was comfortable with, which was to retire at the end of the season.

Decision Making – Sample Dialogue

Coachee: I hadn't realised how much went into getting into the Zone.

Coach: In what way?

Coachee: How much preparation is involved, in particular how many decisions have to be made, some of them deliberate… some of them just as part of being ready. Could I use this for something else I have to deal with, at work, at present?

Coach: Sure, that's a really good way to embed the Zone and make it a more natural process. What is the issue?

Coachee: It's a promotion issue. Normally I would do this intuitively as I believe that's the best way to deal with people.

Coach: Why do you think having a more structured way of making this decision would help?

Coachee: Sometimes I have got it wrong in the past and, with hindsight, I realised it wasn't really intuition. It was flying by the seat of my pants. Also – some structure would make it easier to explain and communicate to my bosses and my people.

Coach: So how would you like to proceed?

Coachee: Not sure. I'm a bit intimidated by the process you have shared with me but it might be a good idea to do all, or part of it, and see what happens.

Coach: That's a good idea, let's have a look at it again and decide how to start. Are you okay with that?

Coachee: I am.

Non-Verbal Communication

QUOTE: In theory there is no difference between theory and practice, in practice there is – Unknown

The reason this section is called non-verbal communication rather than body language is that such terminology provides a much fuller description. When people talk about body language they often simplify it down to a few facial, hand, or body gestures.

Non-verbal communication in this book means everything that is evidenced in the communication; including things like differences in pitch, pace, tonality, emphasis when speaking and things like eye movements, skin colour changes, breathing patterns. All of these are forms of communication which provide a fuller picture than mere words, and which can be helpful in the coaching and Zone contexts. For example the non-verbal communication (NVC) of someone in the Zone is likely to be substantially different to when they are in a normal state.

In this section we will share some of the classic NVC signals based upon many pieces of research and a long history (bear in mind that NVC was used long before language existed). However, the key point is to only use the classic signals as a guide, *always fine tune observations to the individual*. In other words when someone folds their arms it may normally mean that they are being defensive but fine tuning to the individual sometimes indicates something else.

It is therefore really useful for a coach to have an insight into NVC, both to help the coachee but also to help themselves become more self-aware and improve their own effectiveness.

The classic examples of interpreting NVC are as follows:

Receptive	**Defensive**
Sitting forward, relaxed	Crossed arms
Unbuttoned coat	Tightly crossed legs
Legs crossed loosely, relaxed	Tight fists
Slight smile	Hidden hands (pockets)
Hands resting lightly	Hands covering mouth
Open hands/palms	Leg over chair (protecting my territory)
Comfortable eye contact	Sudden/challenging/no eye contact

Key Skills

Confident
Steepling fingers
Strong posture
Less blinking
Hands behind back
Hands behind head
Looking over glasses
Fists on desk (my territory)

Nervous
Shifting body weight
Body trying to escape
More blinking
Clearing throat
Whistling
Ear tugging
Covering mouth while speaking

Readiness
Leaning forward
Positive gestures
Nodding
Standing up
Clear movements

Boredom
Body slouched
Swinging feet
Wandering gaze
Doodling
Fiddling with pen, watch, phone
Drumming fingers
Cupping head in hands

Evaluating
Still
Stroking chin
Polishing glasses
Pacing up and down
Finger on cheek

Doubt/Suspicion
Sideways glance
Touching nose
Rubbing ear
Twisting body
Hand on speaker's arm

Wanting Reassurance
Rubbing hands
Picking fingers
Lint picking
Sucking pen
Pinching fleshy part of hand
Rubbing a personal object e.g. watch or ring

Anger/Frustration
Rubbing back of neck
Jabbing, pointing fingers
Scowling
Throwing down pen
Clenching fists
Running hands through hair

There is a huge amount of information around regarding NVC. However, it is not necessary to go deeper in order to be able to use and respond to non-verbal communication effectively and purposefully. But, remember, it is a key part of the coach's repertoire when looking to help someone optimise their chances of getting into the Zone.

Non-Verbal Communication – Activities

There are a number of well-known techniques for practising non-verbal communication and reading them 'cold' can make them seem slight or even a little manipulative. However, remember that without a positive intent and the skill to 'fine tune' to the individual (or team) these techniques will not work and could possibly change the relationship. Used with integrity they add tremendous value to the quality of the work carried out.

Activity 1

When working with people, socially observe what is called 'the dance of body language'. This means observing when people match or mirror each other (normally a sign of rapport). Equally, observe when people are not getting on and how their non-verbal communication differs.

It's also possible to do this while watching a TV programme (e.g. a debate on Newsnight). In addition it's also a great way to get a lot more out of meetings by directing your attention away from just verbal aspects.

Activity 2

When working with a coachee pay attention to their non-verbal communication and relate it to how effectively the session is going.

Things to look out for:

- how they sit in the chair, their body position, and posture
- failure to maintain good eye contact or overdoing the amount of comfortable eye contact
- unusual patterns in their NVC
- the moment when their NVC changes; what is happening in terms of content at this point?
- unusual hesitations when responding to you
- over-communicating (verbally) their responses
- long, uncomfortable silences

Key Skills

- excessive sighing
- shaking their head

One option when paying attention to a coachee's NVC is to point out what you have observed, without drawing any conclusions, but saying that 'in your experience of working with them' it's unusual.

It is also possible, of course, to draw conclusions and share them with the coachee, although this should be treated with caution. A better option is to share the observation, state how unusual it is, and then tell the coachee how it's making you feel e.g. 'I felt I'd lost your attention when...' or 'I am puzzled by what I have just observed, what are your thoughts?'

Non-Verbal Communication – Case Study

This example may seem fairly trivial and slight - however it was the breakthrough moment in a difficult working relationship.

I was coaching the HR Director of a large multinational company who was known to be a prickly character and who enjoyed having that reputation. I noticed that at the point he was thinking about disagreeing with something I said - he would, dependent on the temperature in his office, stand up, go to the window and either open or close it. Then he would tell me what he disagreed with.

The next time this happened, while he was at the window and before he actually spoke I asked "what the issue was" in what I had said. His behavioural response was what made me think there was an issue as he hadn't actually said anything. I said I thought he had - but not by using words but *by closing the window*. He said my analysis was nonsense it was just that the window needed closing.

I said that may be true but that he opened or closed the window just before verbally disagreeing with me and gave him two other specific examples.

Initially he denied this, then laughed and said he had no idea it was that obvious, then we agreed a way of working together where I needed to alter my style when making key points to him so that he didn't need to open and close the window. We also discussed, and agreed, a more appropriate way for him to respond verbally when I still got it wrong.

Non-Verbal Communication – Case Study – Sport

This is a fairly straightforward example of the impact of non-verbal communication. The circumstances involved a young professional sportsman who was trying to get into the first team. His performances were good without being outstanding and when he wasn't performing well his NVC became visibly negative (i.e. shoulders slumped, he dragged himself around the pitch, looking around and blaming others).

When confronted about this he denied it vehemently and said that the coaches were looking for reasons not to pick him. He also said that none of his team mates had ever said anything about his body language to him, which was true but they *had* said something to the coaches (although it was decided not to tell him this as it was felt that it would distract him from the real issue).

As part of reviewing games (and performances) video analysis was used. As part of the discussion with the coaches about how best to deal with the situation it was decided to have a look at some of the player's performances and his non-verbal communication.

The video analysis confirmed how negative his NVC was and so he was given a copy of the footage, asked to have a look at it, and then be prepared to comment on it at a review meeting. He did this and was astounded by what he saw. He genuinely had not realised and was shocked and mortified by what he saw. He also asked his team mates about it and they confirmed the impact it had on them.

This allowed for a purposeful meeting to take place culminating in plans being put in place to help him deal with the issue.

Non-Verbal Communication – Sample Dialogue

It might seem odd to have some sample dialogue about a topic like Non Verbal Communication! However, it's the best way to make the impact of NVC more explicit.

Coach: What is it - in what I am saying - that you don't like or are struggling to accept?

Coachee: What makes you think there is anything?

Coach: Well there is a pattern I have noticed that always seems to happen when you are about to disagree, or argue, with me.

Coachee: That sounds very unlikely. People always tell me I'm difficult to read.

Coach: That may be true. It's just a small thing I have noticed but it happens on a regular basis.

Coachee: So you think I disagree and argue with you a lot then?

Coach: (laughs) Often enough to spot when it's going to happen.

Coachee: (grins) Go on then.

Coach: Every time you are thinking about how to put across your disagreement, you stand up, go to the window and, depending on the temperature in the room, either open or close the window.

Coachee: That's nonsense. If I disagree with you I just come right out and tell you.

Coach: So how do I know it is coming?

Coachee: That's a valid point. But the real point is that it's not complicated, it's just that the window needs opening or closing.

Coach: So had you noticed it yourself?

Coachee: I knew I'd recognised a change in the room temperature but that's all.

Coach: Any thoughts about why you always seem to notice it when you are just about to disagree with me ?

Coachee: I'm not saying I accept what you are saying but nonetheless it's interesting you've picked up on it.

Coach: If there is something in it, what might it mean?

Coachee: I guess it could be because I'm not sure how to get my point across to you - as we've not worked together for very long.

Coach: Anything else?

Coachee: Well it could also mean that I'm not handling you very well, not getting my point across properly, or not explaining the thinking behind it. It also might mean that I am wrong. (laughs) I hadn't thought of that. So what do we do now?

Coach: For a start let's talk about how I try to get my points across to you and how I can improve that. Then, move on to talk about you, and how you respond.

Coachee: (grins) This sounds like fun, let's give it a go.

Dealing with Self-Limiting Beliefs

QUOTE: Acceptance without proof is the fundamental characteristic of Western religion. Rejection without proof is the fundamental characteristic of Western science – Unknown

This is another of those areas which often crops up in coaching situations particularly in relation to the Zone. Even successful people who appear to be full of confidence and who have a track record of getting things right will, on occasion, limit themselves by not really believing they can do or achieve something. Alternatively they may achieve the Zone occasionally but not believe they can do so on a regular, consistent basis.

There are also, of course, people who are riddled by self-doubt who may in the end come to believe that they (and their lives) are worthless and believe that the Zone does not exist for them. One of the great things about coaching is its focus on the practical. There is obviously a role for, if required, counselling and therapy, however coaching can make a huge difference to the quality of people's lives by encouraging them to adapt their behaviour and their beliefs.

Some examples of self-limiting beliefs are:

- I'll never be able to do...
- I'm not made to be happy
- I'm not clever enough

- I'm not lucky enough
- If only...

Many of these beliefs are rooted in childhood, words parents have used (probably unintentionally), or one specific incident which went badly and has been extended to cover the rest of a lifetime. Some self-limiting beliefs are deeply held and based on repeated patterns, others were born in a few minutes or one incident.

One of the issues with connecting the Zone and self-limiting beliefs is the difficulty in explaining the Zone. Sometimes, even with people who have had amazing experiences of the Zone, they believe it was a fluke and just happened, therefore cannot be repeated - another limiting belief!

There are some coaches who believe that at least one full session, preferably early in the coaching process, should be spent on self-limiting beliefs. My experience is that this is overkill and runs the risk of embedding rather than dealing with them. I find it much more effective to deal with them as they occur and let the coachee learn how deeply they have affected and limited their lives, but that they can be overcome.

The coach's role therefore is to use all of the skills covered in this section and use them in a way that purposefully challenges, not the coachee, but the self-limiting belief. This normally requires:

- that in spite of the belief being challenged the coach still believes in and will support and help the coachee
- the worth/self-esteem of the coachee should be enhanced not violated
- the coach shows respect and understanding for the circumstances that gave birth to the self-limiting belief but still holds consistently that this can be dealt with by moving forward
- the coach, having actually listened, focuses on the future and ways of moving ahead
- the coach does not overdo their own personal examples of dealing with self-limiting beliefs as this can actually build barriers and alienate the coachee, sometimes leading to actually further embedding the self-limiting belief

Many coachees are amazed, some intrigued, some frightened when they realise that self-limiting beliefs can be tackled but that it requires action on their part. Also they are often astounded at how many different approaches and techniques there are to help with this issue. Therefore in this section we will cover a number of techniques in order to provide relevant choices.

Dealing with Self-Limiting Beliefs – Activity 1

This activity, through questioning from the coach, is designed to unpick the issue, reveal the self-limiting belief for what it is, and then provide a future orientation for dealing with it.

1. Take a specific self-limiting belief, in this case, "I am rubbish at presentations and could not get into the Zone while doing one."

2. Answer the following questions

   - How is this belief absurd or ridiculous?

   - What will it ultimately cost me emotionally if I don't let go of this belief?

   - What will it ultimately cost me in my relationships at work if I don't let go of this belief?

   - What will it ultimately cost me physically if I don't let go of this belief?

   - What will it ultimately cost me financially if I don't let go of this belief?

This can seem like a bleak, negative approach but is remarkably powerful as a means of helping coachees face, and act on, their self-limiting beliefs.

Another way to deal with this same issue is…

Dealing with Self-Limiting Beliefs – Activity 2

Issue: "I am rubbish at presentations and could not get into the Zone while doing one."

Stage 1 The coach asks the following questions and notes down the responses:

- because ………

- before ....
- after ....
- while ....
- whenever ....
- so that ....
- if ....
- although ....
- in the same way that ....

Stage 2 The coach asks the same questions but this time based on "I want to be good at presentations and be able to get into the Zone while doing one."

- because ....
- other questions as above.

Stage 3 The coach asks the same questions but this time based on "I will be good at presentations and be able to get into the Zone."

- because ....
- other questions as above.

This can seem drawn out and repetitive but this needs to be explained to the coachee; the benefits and positive change achieved in beliefs and behaviour can be life changing.

Dealing with Self-Limiting Beliefs – Activity 3

This, again, is a well-known and used technique and can be used in the coaching session or as a 'task' to be carried out separately. It's known as the A-F model and is based on the famous A-B-C model used in Cognitive Behaviour and Rational Emotive Behaviour Therapy for many years. I have found this to be one of the most effective tools in the coach's toolbox and really good when used in connection with the Zone.

Its purpose needs to be explained to the coachee beforehand and a specific aspect chosen (e.g. the same one as Activity 2 "I am rubbish at presentations and could not get into the Zone while doing one.")

The Steps:

A. What is the *activity* event? (e.g. the presentations issue)
B. What is the self-limiting *belief* about the event?

   - "I know I'm rubbish and so does everybody else."

C. What are the *consequences* of this belief:

   - "I will confirm to myself and others that I am rubbish."

D. How can I *dispute* the self-limiting belief? E.g. how real is this belief? What can I *do* to overcome it? Is perfection really necessary? Can I practise getting into the Zone beforehand?
E. What are more *effective* new beliefs? E.g. it's all in my own head – I have given good presentations previously – It's good to be nervous and want to get it right – If I practise well I can have a good shot at this – When have I been in the Zone when not presenting?
F. What new *feelings* do I now have? E.g. I am prepared to give it a go – It will be brilliant to get it right – It will be great to prove myself wrong.

This works really well face-to-face but then I would suggest the coachee takes a blank copy of this away to work on.

When following up on this, focus - in particular - on Steps D-F

- *disputing* the self-limiting belief by asking purposeful, open, probing questions
- agreeing with the coachee *effective* new empowering beliefs
- dealing with the new *feelings* with the coachee agreeing to, and committing to, actions that will enable them to do something live, e.g. give a presentation, do a dummy run with colleagues, friends, their partner, you as their coach.

Review and plan for ongoing action.

Dealing with Self-Limiting Beliefs – Case Study

This example centred around a female manager who felt that she wasn't being treated equally with her male colleagues. Her way of dealing with it was to become louder and more forthright and aggressive. Inevitably this tended to prolong the issue rather than solve it.

At our initial sessions she insisted that it was all down to the 'glass ceiling' and the envy of her colleagues. The way she repeatedly put this argument forward hinted at a little of 'she doth protest too much'.

The tricky point was that as her coach I was in danger of being labelled in a similar vein to the males that she worked with. So as part of the coaching I asked her about her relationships with other males. Actually by asking the question I really meant other previous male working colleagues.

At this point she became quite emotional - unusual for her - and told me all about her upbringing with her father and brothers, where she had, she believed, been treated like a little girl and even to this day felt it still happened.

At that session I decided not to pursue matters further but told her that everyone carries some form of self-limiting belief and I wondered what hers might be. She then launched back into berating her male colleagues, not mentioning the males in her family. In spite of having previously decided not to go any further at this session I thought that now was the right time to deal with the situation and gently reminded her of the connections she had made a few minutes ago and asked her if she thought they were relevant.

As frequently happens - she had a 'lightbulb' moment and told me that the thought had never occurred to her before. Avoiding the temptation to delve further I asked her to consider whether she would like to work through a process that could help deal with this; and to let me know before the next session so I could prepare.

This is what she did and at the next session we worked through Activity B and I explained how Activity C worked and she chose to do that one as well. The results of this process were a significant change in her behaviour with her male colleagues and more fruitful relationships with them.

Dealing with Self-Limiting Beliefs – Case Study – Sport

A Professional Golfer had gone through a period when his performances had deteriorated and his earnings had been substantially reduced. This had happened at the point of starting a family which increased the pressure on him to sort it out.

One consequence of this was that his long held, but well hidden, doubts about his true ability had been brought back to the forefront of his mind.

In considering how to deal with this I was unsure about how best to proceed. A colleague suggested I use the 5 step approach outlined in the main body of this section, which I subsequently did.

- I assured him that I was challenging his self-limiting belief because I believed (and the evidence supported the view) that he was a genuinely talented player who was just going through a bad period.
- By asking questions and having evidence I established that, in fact, he should be proud of his achievements and his ability to overcome difficulties.
- Through this approach I was able to demonstrate that I understood the self-limiting belief and how it had come about; I wasn't critical of it, I saw it as normal, but that it could be dealt with.
- We were then able to focus on solutions (e.g. re-visualise past successes, use these to re-anchor triggers to be used in the future, and set some realistic targets for the next three months).
- I avoided falling into the trap of, without meaning to, embedding the negative beliefs I was trying to help him overcome

The outcome of this interaction was him committing to a plan to deal with the issue and over the next three months, without being a world beater, he was able to get back to the level he had decided would prove he could be successful.

Dealing With Self-Limiting Beliefs – Sample Dialogue

This Sample Dialogue is part of a coaching for the Zone session using Activity 1.

Coach: So, what is the specific belief you wanted to go a bit further into?

Coachee: I guess it's quite a common one. It's about not being good at presentations and believing that I won't be able to get into the Zone when I do one.

Key Skills

Coach: Tell me a bit more about it.

[A detailed conversation takes place regarding the history of the coachee, presentations, and the Zone.]

Coach: Okay, so how is this belief absurd or ridiculous?

Coachee: It's stupid really. I always get good feedback, I seem to able to deal with the questions okay and I normally keep getting asked to do presentations. Plus my line manager told me I was good at them at my last appraisal.

Coach: If you don't change this belief what will the cost be emotionally?

Coachee: It will continue to drain my energy and affect my view about myself.

Coach: What will it cost you in your relationships?

Coachee: I guess it will mean that people will not consider me as competent, or as mentally strong, as I would like them to.

Coach: What will it cost you physically?

Coachee: Loss of energy, poor sleep, feeling down all the time.

Coach: And financially?

Coachee: I'm not sure, but it could be career limiting.

Coach: How does this belief of yours look now?

Coachee: Actually, I realised about halfway through this conversation that it looks and feels pretty trivial.

Coach: So what would you like to do about it?

Dealing With Emotions

QUOTE: No-one can go back and make a brand new start, but anyone can start right now and make a brand new ending – Unknown

This can be one of the most difficult aspects of coaching with regard to the Zone mainly because the Zone often leads to people's emotional levels being heightened - putting them in a different state to normal. This is most often seen in sport, when players, managers and coaches often seem to be 'outside themselves' with joy or satisfaction. This can be exactly the same in any other context as well.

This dynamic effect of the Zone is, of course, one of the reasons why it is so powerful and why it has such a large impact. One of the points that makes this so intriguing is that this is normally the aftermath of the Zone, because while actually in it everything is happening effortlessly and outside of time so everything is under control (but unconsciously).

One further factor in dealing with emotions is that the coaching process itself can be emotional, often for the coachee and sometimes for both parties. There are a number of reasons for this, one being the open, deep, and life changing aspects of coaching.

Another is that it is not unusual for the breakthrough in the coaching process to be achieved when emotions become involved.

I work mainly in the corporate world where a lot of what happens is based on logic, rational thought, and hard data and the coaching process normally starts using 360° feedback, competencies, and performance management systems. This is really important as it fits with how the managers would normally operate, however the key issue is often an emotional one rather than a rational one. For example getting promoted (or not), a particularly difficult relationship, not being able to take people with you.

Often the emotional moment comes 'out of the blue' with little obvious sign that it is coming. The chances of seeing it coming are increased by using the skills covered in this section, in particular the reading of non-verbal communication. However there will still be many occasions when - out of nowhere - it is suddenly there and the coachee is probably more surprised than the coach!

The key at this point is for the coach not to overreact or change what they are doing. Any change of style or emphasis at this point is likely to lose or damage both the moment and/or relationship.

Therefore remaining calm and focused and acting as though everything is a rational consequence of the discussion is absolutely vital.

Dealing With Emotions – Case Study

The context for this case study was a senior manager in a large organisation who had been consistently successful and promoted. Recently he had applied for a job within the company and, to his total surprise, both not got the job but also lost it to someone who currently reported to him.

At this point the manager was in his mid-forties, and the person who got the job in his mid-thirties. The Manager saw this as both a generational change and a changing of the guard. In other words, he viewed events as the end of his career with still another 15-20 years of a working life left to complete.

In the next coaching session he was, initially, slightly quieter than usual, then as the session went on he became increasingly volatile. He did not specifically talk about the missed promotion, more about some fairly mundane information and data he had to produce for a meeting.

I was faced with carrying on in this style or introducing the missed promotion to get his reaction.

In a neutral way I dealt with the issue of the meeting then asked him if anything else of importance had occurred since we last met. His initial response was to mention the missed promotion briefly, be matter-of-fact about the situation, and explain why the company had made the decision it had. Partway through this the way he spoke and the types of words he used changed; he became more personal and emotional and he mentioned unfairness and how he was considering his future.

At this point I asked him how he actually 'felt' about the situation and this set off quite a long speech which became the most emotional I had ever seen him give. This was obviously a key issue for him so I let him talk only asking questions for clarification and then letting him continue. There came a point where he 'ran out of steam' a little and we put a plan together for the next few coaching sessions so that he could again demonstrate his performance and competence.

Dealing With Emotions – Activity

1. Learn to classify emotions (both yours and the coachee's) rather than complicating things by putting emotional labels on their emotional responses (e.g. "They look bored therefore they don't like me.") Be aware as Hamlet said, "Nothing that happens is either good or bad but thinking makes it so."

   The classic patterns to look out for are:

   - Sadness
   - Fear
   - Shame
   - Anger
   - Guilt
   - Denial
   - Jealousy

   Spotting the pattern is a helpful step to emotional distance and helping to create time to think about an appropriate response.

2. The next stage is consider the following guidelines:

   - emotions are not necessarily true, false, harmful, relevant or true
   - emotions often argue against themselves
   - we are responsible for our own reactions when someone displays emotions we recognise and accept
   - we are also responsible for our actions when someone displays emotions which we recognise but don't accept

3. Respond with one or more of the following techniques:

   - label the emotion/ask the coachee to label the emotion
   - use a delay to the emotion
   - ask the coachee on the effect of the emotion
   - ask probing questions to establish the trigger for the emotion
   - ask the coachee to consider the benefits/problems having the emotion could cause
   - ask the coachee to redefine the emotion

- move to a solution rather than focus on the problem
- get them to anchor a more effective solution

Dealing With Emotions – Case Study – Sport

Unsurprisingly there is a lot of emotion attached to sport! However, it would be wrong to think that there is no emotion involved in the world of business. It is often hidden by a cognitive approach, but it is always there in some form or other.

This case study involves a captain of a club who had been appointed because of his experience and background (i.e. his International career and his high levels of personal performance). The club was aware that his appointment was a little controversial as he had never been the greatest team player and did things his own way.

At the pre-season team building session he was very clear regarding the standards he expected surrounding issues such as time keeping, dress codes, levels of preparation, etc. At the end of his input he asked if there were any questions and didn't get any response. After the session I asked him how he thought it had gone and what his reaction to not being asked any questions was. His response was that it meant that everybody was on-board with him and everything was okay.

Subsequently as the season got under way the team started badly, losing games that they should not have. His response was to crack the whip even harder and give individual players, and the team in general, a hard time. This culminated in a situation where one of the players actually cried because they felt they were being victimised and picked on unfairly.

At this point the captain asked me to sit in on a session with the player and asked me my thoughts on how he should prepare. My initial response was to ask him how he intended playing it and he showed me all the data and evidence he had prepared to prove his point. I then asked how he intended to deal with any emotions that might arise and he responded that if he managed the session properly emotions would not arise. I then asked him again what he would do if they did and he repeated that they wouldn't.

I then considered how best I could help both the captain and the player and thought of the activity covered in this section; I asked him if he was willing to have a look at it. Somewhat grudgingly he agreed and we went through it. Having done this he said he thought it was 'soft' and 'namby pamby'. I responded that it might look that way but, in my experience, it was actually much harder than just laying the law down because it actually engaged the other person. I asked him which parts of the approach might be the most useful and he said that he liked the part about emotions not necessarily being true/false, and also the part about labelling the emotion.

At the player meeting, the captain started as he had planned to and the player responded as he had previously (becoming emotional). To my total surprise, instead of carrying on with his approach, the captain stopped the meeting and explained what he was trying to achieve and why he had chosen to do it that way. He also labelled his own emotions regarding the fact that his approach was obviously not working and asked the player to label his own emotions. After an uncomfortable few minutes the player did this and the meeting was able to move forward in a more positive way.

Dealing With Emotions – Sample Dialogue

Coach: How did you feel about not getting the job you wanted?

Coachee: [Talks for some time.]

Coach: In your view what is the real issue here?

Coachee: Initially I thought it was about not getting the job… but if I'm honest a lot of it is that one of my reports got it instead.

Coach: Why is that such a big deal?

Coachee: Because it might mean I've had my chance!

Coach: How does that make you feel?

Coachee: How long have you got? Annoyed, irritated, neglected, ignored, not rated.

Coach: Which of these are the big ones?

Coachee: Hmmm, I suppose being not rated.

Coach: Why?

Coachee: Because it means everything I have done is worthless.

Coach: In what way?

Coachee: If I was rated I would have got the job.

Coach: Really?

Coachee: Maybe that's not really right.

Coach: So what's a better way to express it?

Coachee: Perhaps it's a wake-up call for me.

Coach: In what way?

Coachee: Perhaps I have been cruising a bit, and not really pushing myself.

Coach: So what's the best way to respond to this situation?

Coachee: Not get side-tracked by this, knuckle down, focus on what needs to be done – basically just get on with it.

Intuition

QUOTE: People demand freedom of speech as a compensation for the freedom of thought which they seldom use – Kierkegaard

Like many aspects of both coaching and the Zone, intuition is either a piece of magic, blindingly obvious, or complete bunkum. In other words it's something that can appear obvious and easy or something that is too abstract to be relevant.

The Webster's Dictionary definition of intuition is – *the act of power or direct or immediate knowledge – instinctive knowledge*. This latter definition rings true in so many aspects of life, particularly when it comes to people; the sports manager who chooses one player before another or who signs a new player, the manager at work who promotes someone, a crowd of friends which (normally unspoken) allows someone to join them as a friend.

A good case could be made that nearly all the big decisions in life involve a degree of intuition. Try asking someone why they fell in love with a particular person and, often, the response will be 'it just felt right'. Definitely a form of 'instinctive knowledge'.

Recently many studies in the Neurosciences, particularly around the plasticity of the brain, have been carried out regarding this topic and further work is still going on into this fascinating subject. The evidence of this research suggests that the brain is not 'fixed' but can adapt and modify itself to deal with different problems and situations by using different parts of itself.

Certainly the ability to 'read' people and situations is one factor that can make the power of coaching, and the Zone, so powerful and yet it is often not mentioned in any of the literature. One reason for this is that, at the present time, it is extremely difficult to train someone to improve their intuition, so you won't see it mentioned in training course programmes. I have yet to see an MBA programme that has a module on intuition!

The anomaly here is that intuition impacts on virtually all our major decisions from buying a new car to changing our jobs, yet a lot of people feel that they are not good at intuition but they know someone who is extremely good at reading people and/or situations.

One anecdotal definition I heard many years ago is that "intuition is the sum of our prior experiences". My interpretation of this is that intuition doesn't just fly in through the open door of our brain like magic dust and provide the right answer. It's not just random. The foundation for it is everything we have done before but there is still the element of the unknown that 'feels right' or 'it's a gut feel'.

A problem with intuition is that it can, of course, be wrong! No-one gets it right every time. One reason for this is that often the areas where intuition is applied are the more ambiguous ones, where there is not necessarily a concrete black and white answer.

It's important to remember that when we use our intuition we are making an interpretation, not a concrete judgement. Even people with outstanding intuitive skills can sometimes forget this and act as though their reading of a person/situation is 100% right. In coaching it is particularly vital not to have a vested interest in 'being right'. Therefore one skill is to say "My feeling is..." or

"My guess is that there is something else happening here". The tricky part is to use intuition to open up and probe something, but not to treat it as 'solid gold'.

Equally of course, even if the coach has well-developed intuition skills they are inevitably going to meet a coachee who is actually better at it than they are. Rather than compete or withdraw - the coach should welcome it and, where appropriate, nurture and further develop it.

Yet in spite of all this, intuition is often the key factor that makes the difference in coaching, the Zone, and in life itself.

In the context of the Zone, because of the nature of the experience (in particular the unconscious competence aspect) it is the ability to process information, make decisions. and do what feels right that is likely to make the difference.

Intuition – Activity

The purpose of this activity is to provide a safe framework for helping to bring out your coachee's skills of intuition. It's called the 'best guess'.

- sit with a friend or colleague and ask them about some aspect of their life; it could be a job, hobby, being a parent – the less you know about the topic the better.
- use the 'do's and 'don't's of questioning, in particular the open, probing questions *but* don't get hung up on this or start to analyse their responses in terms of content; totally resist the temptation to provide answers to whatever is being put forward.
- pay particular notice to their powerful non-verbal communication, e.g. posture, gestures, breathing, skin colour changes, eye contact.
- allow yourself to see the whole person in front of you, freewheel your thoughts, encourage (don't suppress) random, disconnected thoughts.
- at a point that feels right say 'my best guess about how you feel about this is...'
- if the natural moment for 'my best guess' doesn't arrive... *do it anyway*, even though, logically, you have no idea what you are going to say (remember you are with a friend!)
- suspend logic and just go with 'my best guess is you are feeling...'
- don't look to be *right*; remember it is your best guess and best guesses might be wrong. It's actually about developing and pushing your intuitive

abilities.
- try this on irregular, random occasions in real life situations e.g. social and work.
- if helpful, look for patterns when your intuition is consistently accurate e.g. certain people and/or situations, and also when it is less accurate
- review – what is your *intuition* telling you about these patterns?

Intuition – Case Study

Coaching and the Zone frequently offer opportunities to use intuition and it often provides the breakthrough 'aha' moment for the coachee.

In this example the coachee (a Research Scientist) was constantly finding that, at work, he was regularly feeling left out, or behind. The scientist always required lots of data which was fine in terms of his day-to-day lab work but slowed everything down when he attended management meetings where he was expected to make recommendations based on the data.

In unpicking this issue it was apparent that he was scared of putting the wrong decision forward and letting down the scientific community. He also felt, to some extent, out of his depth at the meetings as the others seemed to have a much broader knowledge of the business but were willing to make decisions without having all the data or, sometimes, in spite of the data.

Further discussion revealed the point that intuition wasn't real science and it was really 'making it up as you go along'. Rather than deal with this in the specific work situation, I asked the coachee about his experience of situations outside work including family and friends.

His answer was that he often felt out of his depth in knowing how to deal with his children. He tried to be logical, fair and consistent but his wife seemed to be able to read situations differently and better. So, whenever they discussed these topics he once more was 'wrong'… he just hadn't got it.

As the conversation developed he also mentioned that he was a fisherman and at this point his physiology changed, along with his words and speed and the emphasis in his speech. We had never discussed the Zone in our coaching sessions but I asked him to describe how it felt when he made the right decisions when he was fishing. What he described was his version of the Zone and what produced it was him making the right decision and, normally landing the fish.

It had never occurred to him that although he had data and previous experience to use, he was also actually making his fishing decisions based upon his own intuition (i.e. instinctive knowledge). We then discussed a) that he actually did have intuition and b) could he take this into the workplace? He still felt uncomfortable with doing it regarding the data in meetings but agreed to try it by observing the process/dynamics of the meeting (i.e. how he 'felt' it was going).

As a further step we agreed that he initially would do this without sharing his observations, we would review them in the coaching sessions, but that the mid-term goal was for him to make an observation or 'best guess' actually in a meeting and see what happened.

The outcome of this came in the third meeting. Much to the coachee's surprise, the other attendees agreed with him and didn't seem surprised by what he had pointed out.

Intuition – Case Study – Sport

Intuition inevitably plays a large part in many aspects of life and sport is no exception. In fact many managers and coaches consider it one of their greatest skills, often used to justify unusual or controversial team selections and/or how best the team should actually play. Equally many sportspeople talk about their ability to read a game or situation and use their intuition in order to respond effectively.

In this case study intuition was actually used by a coach to explain - to his colleagues - why he wanted to pursue a particular player who was coming towards the end of his career. The coach's view was that he thought the player had one or two more seasons in him and it was worth the risk. His colleagues took a different view but knew that the coach had a good track record in picking players and so, after some debate, they went along with it. The player turned out be successful and actually played on for two further years.

Curiosity

QUOTE: The third rate mind is only happy when it is thinking with the majority. The second rate mind is only happy when it is thinking with the minority. The first rate mind is only happy when it is thinking – Unknown

It may well have killed the cat but curiosity definitely enhances the effectiveness of coaching… especially when it comes to the Zone.

Within coaching it's vital that the coach has a strong sense of curiosity as it enables them to always be fresh and interested in different aspects of the subject and skills of coaching as well as the various types of people they will be coaching. There is nothing worse than rolling out the same old process, in the same old way, irrespective of the situation or coachee.

Equally when it comes to the Zone it's difficult to imagine a coachee being able to get into the Zone unless some degree of curiosity is involved. It could be about the coach, the process, outcomes, or what difference it would make to be able to achieve the Zone on a more regular, consistent basis. It could be argued that this sense of curiosity is vital to being able to achieve the Zone as it is part of being open to new and different experiences.

Many coaches would argue that curiosity must be present at the first stage for true learning to occur and for the coachee to be able to get into the Zone. Therefore creating a climate where curiosity flourishes can be very powerful.

Curiosity – Activity

The great thing about curiosity, as with all interpersonal skills, is that it doesn't need to be practised alone in a darkened room. It works best when done with or among others, even if they don't know what we are doing.

A well-known activity is to be in a public place, put your attention outwards, and initially observe what is happening around you. Start by noticing movement and the rhythm of people moving then notice the words (not the content but the volume, ebb and flow). Then tune into the actual words and see what you notice.

When you feel the moment is right (intuition) ask someone a question about something they have said. Don't feel embarrassed or afraid, but engage with the other person (people) until you find something out you didn't know before.

Within the next 24 hours initiate a conversation with someone completely different and unconnected and manage to find a way to introduce your new piece of knowledge or observation then see what you learn about it from this new person.

Curiosity – Case Study

I was reminded of how powerful the natural curiosity of children is recently when talking to the 8 year old daughter of some friends. The girl was asking question after question about the new place they were shortly going to on holiday.

The parents, harassed about the planning for the trip, tried to be positive and helpful but essentially wanted the girl to be quiet or at least ask the questions at a point they were more able to be receptive to (which, of course, might never happen).

This seemingly trivial incident reminded me of how naturally curious children are, and how important it is to their development. Also that adults, in general, tend to discourage children from being curious as it doesn't suit the time or the mood of the adult rather than foster and nurture the child's further development.

Curiosity – Sample Dialogue

Coach: How did you get on at the meeting we discussed at the last session?

Coachee: It was really interesting but not in the way I was expecting.

Coach: That sounds intriguing…

Coachee: It wasn't really about the stuff that was on the agenda. It was about how the people interacted with each other.

Coach: Go on.

Coachee: It was like two meetings going on. One based on the words said and one based on the unspoken part.

Coach: Tell me more.

Coachee: [Elaborates.]

Coach: So why did this impact on you so much?

Coachee: It made me curious about why I had suddenly started to pick up on this.

Coach: And?

Coachee: I think it's because of our chats about the Zone that I'm starting to notice things like this. They were obviously happening all along.

Coach: How can you build on, and develop, this curiosity?

Coachee: I can make a deliberate effort to use it and then trust my intuition to respond as to how best to use it.

Coach: Good idea. When is your next opportunity to practice your curiosity?

Assisting Learning

Like many aspects of coaching and the Zone the idea of assisting learning sounds blindingly obvious. How could a coach not help the coachee learn? And how could the coachee not want to learn more about themselves and how to improve their performance?

An interesting point about this is that, although the answers to the questions above ought be a resounding yes - it doesn't always work out that way. People's reluctance to change habits and ways of doing things should not be underestimated. So a major part of the coach's job is 'unblocking' unhelpful approaches and helping the coachee move forward.

It's also possible for the coach to be the one that requires 'unblocking'; a coach's need for constant vigilance and self-awareness should not be underestimated.

One other quirk regarding learning should also be noted. Often one of the key blocks is not at the beginning (which is subsequently overcome before everything becomes plain sailing!), rather it's surprisingly common that a change is made, progress achieved, learning takes place, and *then* the coachee sticks at that point rather than push on. It's as though, in spite of having demonstrated to themselves, and often others, that they can go beyond anything they have ever achieved before, they get frightened by the vastness of the unknown. Self-limiting barriers appear and they back off. This may sound counter-intuitive, but it is a regular occurrence, even in management or professional sport where you would least expect it.

A separate point is how the coach helps the coachee learn. Although there are a number of models of learning, the coach needs to be perceptive and flexible enough to avoid committing to only one approach.

Zeus and Skiffington (2002) make the following points regarding learning and performance. Coaches should be aware of:

- the type of learning they wish to foster
- what the coachee will gain from the intervention
- any underlying assumptions they have regarding learning

They also make the following useful points regarding coaching for learning and coaching for performance.

- learning tends to focus on what is happening inside the individual, whereas performance has its focus on the outside work environment
- learning involves or increases the individual's knowledge, skills and abilities whereas performance is a function of the individual's competence in the workplace
- learning is about new information, assumptions, beliefs and feelings that produce changes to the individual's entire way of being in the world. Performance can be measured against external, behavioural standards.

Some of this can sound a little semantic, however it is important for the coach and coachee to be aware of the distinctions. This is particularly true regarding the Zone because it's really powerful for the coachee to see that they can achieve both learning *and* performance improvements by working on the Zone.

There can be a tendency to assume that learning is always a positive experience, yet most of us know that we have learnt as much, sometimes more, from failure. Due to the nature of learning, failure (however defined) will frequently occur and

142

needs to be dealt with, particularly with something like the Zone.

Therefore some failures along the way will be part of the roadmap to success, but this may well depend on how the coach and in particular the coachee deal with it. Again it may sound counter-intuitive but being able to deal with, respond to, and learn from failure is vital. Sport is an obvious place where this occurs, but it is important in all walks of life.

Assisting Learning – Activity

Most coaches will be familiar with a variety of learning models. Coaches need to be aware of their learning preferences provided they don't become slavish to them or assume their own preference is either 'right' or 'universal'.

Probably the best known framework in the UK is Dr Peter Honey's – *Learning Styles Inventory*. This inventory gives feedback based on the balance between being an Activist, Pragmatist, Theorist and Reflector and makes the important point that one is not necessarily better than another. There is also a lot of interesting research around the LSI regarding job preferences and other issues based on Learning Styles.

The activity for this section is for the coachee to have a knowledge of various models of learning and to carry out the LSI.

Assisting Learning – Case Study

This case study happened a number of years ago early in my career as a coach. Before I got more formally into coaching I spent many years designing and running management training courses.

These were normally on topics such as influencing, negotiations, dealing with difficult people, leadership, team building. In essence, I focused on the interpersonal skills involved in dealing with people.

This particular coachee was someone who had attended a number of my courses as part of his company's Management Training Programme. On one of the courses I had started with the Learning Styles Inventory (LSI) to help set the scene for the week. As ever this created a lot of debate regarding the accuracy and potential use of these types of instruments.

This had taken place about five years before I started to coach the individual, who had always been challenging both in terms of content and style and had been very strong in his dislike of the feedback from the LSI.

Fast forward five years, and in preparing for the first session I'd visited all my notes from the courses and my other dealings with the individual. I came across his LSI results. I decided to have them available in case they proved helpful. I also decided that, although this could be dangerous, I needed to revisit our previous dealings as part of establishing ground rules for how we would work together.

At the first session we discussed what he wanted to get out of the coaching and one of the things he said was that as a rock climber, cyclist, and tri-athlete he was aware of the Zone and had experienced it on occasions. He wanted to work on taking this into his work as a manager. In discussing this I asked him about the Zone and whether he had realised, at the time, that he was in the Zone. His reply was "No" because he was totally locked into the moment; it was only afterwards he had realised.

In probing this further I remembered that his LSI preferences were for Activist and Pragmatist and he had come out as low on Reflector. I reminded him of this and, instead of becoming defensive, he laughed and said that he realised this. He went on to say that, although it wasn't his natural preference, when he really learnt something (and responded to learning) it always seemed to be based on him pondering and reflecting afterwards. We were then able to introduce and plan for reflection to be included in our coaching sessions.

Assisting Learning – Case Study – Sport

As with curiosity it would be reasonable to expect that managers, coaches and even players would be interested in assisting their colleagues in their learning. Again, although this obviously does happen, it doesn't happen to the extent that might be expected!

Often with the Zone, partly because it can be seen as unique to an individual, it is often ignored, left to chance, or taken for granted. As part of the research for this book I spoke with dozens of coaches from a wide variety of sports about how they went about assisting people's learning regarding the Zone and met with a range of reactions - very few of which involved approaching the Zone in a structured, coherent way.

Some examples of where it was tackled, albeit it in a fairly haphazard way, involved coaches who got players to review specific, high performing examples of where an individual had exceeded themselves, and got them to re-live the experience and analyse it to see what they had done and what they could do to repeat it. This normally was as far as it went.

It is hoped that those who read this book will implement approaches that create and allow for learning to be embedded and repeated on an ongoing basis.

Assisting Learning – Sample Dialogue

Coach: …That's interesting, so when you are rock climbing and in the Zone you don't actually realise it at the time?

Coachee: That's right, I only realise afterwards. Is that normal?

Coach: Absolutely. How do you know, afterwards, that you were in the Zone?

Coachee: What do you mean?

Coach: Do you do a structured review with yourself?

Coachee: More like a semi-organised reflection.

Coach: Have you always done that?

Coachee: Not really, but when I do - it's really helpful.

Coach: That's worth knowing. Do you remember when you did the course and we did the Learning Styles Inventory?

Coachee: (laughs) Oh yes. I was very awkward about it as I recall.

Coach: (smiles) Well, you certainly made your views clear. What do you remember?

Coachee: I argued about the relevance and accuracy of these sort of inventories.

Key Skills

And, in particular, my results.

Coach: And?

Coachee: I've realised, since, that I am definitely an Activist/Pragmatist so I was right about that. But when I really learn it's when I ponder and think a bit more about things afterwards. This was really important with the Zone.

Coach: That's a really powerful bit of learning. How can we use that moving forward, particularly with regard to the Zone?

Using Appropriate Language Patterns

Most people tend to focus on content (i.e. what is actually being said about the subject) when considering language. However, the types of words and how those words are said carries just as much, if not more, information.

A lot of work has been carried out in the field of Neuro-Linguistic Programming (NLP) regarding language patterns based on the five senses (visual, auditory, kinaesthetic (emotions and muscular), olfactory (smell) and gustatory (taste)).

One of the key learning points is that, depending on the individual's dominance/preference towards the five senses - their language will alter accordingly. The classic breakdown regarding these sensory words is:

Visual: focus, clear, image, bright, view, picture, insight, hazy, vivid, dim, look, dark, vision, perspective, transparent, reflect, outlook, shady

Auditory: click, resonate, rhythm, hearsay, wavelength, tone, harmony, loud, language, clash, tune, call, accent, say, question

Kinaesthetic: smooth, thrust, texture, touch, warm, rub, pushy, contact, sticky, itch, pressure, rough, flow, shining, move, weight

Olfactory: whiff, reek, smell, stagnant, acrid, fragrant, stink, scent, rancid, fresh, cheesy

Gustatory: sweet, taste, flavour, sour, bitter, choke, chew, swallow, bland, bite, juicy

So, for example, someone could be an accountant and their verbalised content would be about figures, profit, loss, balance sheets, and capital expenditure - but the sensory words within any description would be significantly biased towards their preferences within the five senses.

In the section on Non-Verbal Communication we discussed how posture, gestures, smiles, and more, can be matched and mirrored when people are in rapport and getting on. The same applies with the use of sensory language. It can also explain why people cannot get along even when, in terms of content, they are talking about the same thing.

Using Appropriate Language Patterns – Activity

1. Listen for the types of sensory words used by a coachee. Match their language patterns but, obviously, use different words from the same sensory pattern.
2. When it is difficult to work out why your verbal communication seems not to be working, pay attention to the sensory descriptions the coachee is using and respond accordingly.

Using Appropriate Language Patterns – Case Study

I was working with a teacher who was extremely passionate about her work and I was trying to demonstrate to her that I could genuinely feel her passion. However the more I tried to do this the more she seemed to be moving away from me and telling me how 'I just couldn't see what her vision was and what she was trying to focus on'.

I realised at this point that she was using predominantly visual language to explain her enthusiasm and I was responding with mainly kinaesthetic (i.e. "I feel really in touch with what you are trying to do.") No matter how well intentioned, it was the wrong use of language that was causing the mix up in the communication.

Therefore the gap in communication between us was not about the content of the discussion, it was a clash (unwittingly) of verbal communication styles (see sample dialogue).

Using Appropriate Language Patterns – Case Study – Sport

In many sports, and not just those dominated by males, the language tends to be combative, almost military and full of exhortation (e.g. try harder, do more (or less), this is war, fight to the end). Sometimes, of course, this is entirely appropriate and has its place. More often than not, however, it doesn't engage hearts and minds and bypasses people and how they like to be communicated with.

An example of this is the team pep talk sometimes carried out before a game or performance, sometimes at an interval, and sometimes at the end. These well intended, and often passionately delivered 'motivational' talks normally tend to say more about the manager, coach or captain than they say about what individuals/the team needs.

An exception to this was a coach I worked with who was a big fan of the Zone and believed it could be achieved virtually at will. His way of delivering his pep talk about the Zone was to use questions, reflective language (e.g. think about a time when), and a mix of all five sensory systems (focussing mainly on the visual, auditory, and in particular the kinaesthetic forms of words and phrases).

When I asked him about this he said he had honed this approach over the years and had found, particularly with the Zone, that although he didn't use exactly the right language for all people all the time - he was 'getting it right for most of the people most of the time'.

Using Appropriate Language Patterns – Sample Dialogue

Coach: How do you feel about your role as a teacher?

Coachee: I am clear about it. It's you that doesn't really seem to see it.

Coach: I know. I'm trying to. But I feel stuck… as though I am digging a pit for myself.

Coachee: I can see that. You don't really see my vision for my life and work do you?

Coach: Ah. So clear this up for me   and help me focus on what I need to

148

do – to get a picture of you in the Zone fulfilling your life and being a teacher.

Coachee: It's all about being able to see myself contributing and being transparent in my role as a teacher.

Coach: So, from your perspective, it's important that you can focus on your vision but also be able to reflect on it and be clear about it.

Coachee: Yes, that's right.

Using Metaphors and Storytelling

Rather like curiosity, the use of metaphors and storytelling is often either consciously ignored or actively discouraged as people grow up. The irony of this is that their use often 'lights fires' in people's minds to create the memorable experiences that impact on people's lives. We often remember stories from childhood but then don't build on their impact.

A coach can use metaphors and storytelling to make a powerful point to a coachee, or a coachee describing an experience (e.g. the Zone) that can motivate someone else to try something they have always wanted to do. This can even come from a television interview (for example, watching Andy Murray after winning Wimbledon, or a favoured celebrity describing their feelings after achieving a major success).

Normally the coach should expect to build on and encourage the metaphors used by the coachee. Sometimes it is the coach who provides any metaphor(s) but again based on something provided by the coachee, not just their own favourite example or story. The coach can do this to help unblock an issue the coachee is having, then sit back and use questions, listening, curiosity and intuition to move things forward.

The other major advantage of using metaphors and storytelling is that they enable the coach to make points, challenge things, be oblique (but still make a point) without creating or embedding barriers in the coachee. It is very difficult to get defensive or argue against a metaphor or story. This then encourages the coachee to push further, take an extra (realistic but challenging) risk by being enthused, and become willing to commit to trying new things.

A cautionary note is that there can be a gap in interpretation between the coach and the coachee regarding any meaning within a metaphor or story. Avoid falling into this trap. Normally go with the coachee's version provided it enables and empowers them.

Some examples of day-to-day metaphors include: "I feel I am swimming against the tide", "I am in a complete fog regarding this", "snug as bug on a rug", "food for thought". These sorts of phrases bypass the conscious mind and communicate directly with the unconscious, which is really the driver for most of our behaviours. They are also incredibly revealing about key issues, thoughts, and challenges.

Based on the five senses covered in the section on Using Appropriate Language Patterns, here is a short list of some metaphors for each of the five senses.

Visual

- Things are looking up
- The outlook is dim
- I can see your point
- I can see right through them
- They have a blind spot
- Turn a blind eye
- Clear as mud

Auditory

- Quiet as a mouse
- On the same wavelength
- Sounds good
- Calling the time
- Strikes a chord
- Ding-dong row
- Rings a bell

Kinaesthetic (Emotions and Physical Feelings)

- Pull yourself together
- Rubs me up the wrong way
- Hat headed
- Get a grip on yourself
- They are a wet blanket

- Solid as a rock
- Doesn't feel right

Olfactory (Smell)

- Smell a rat
- Sniffing around
- Twitching nostrils
- Spilt milk
- Got a nose for the situation

Gustatory (Taste)

- Hard to swallow
- Leaves a nasty taste in the mouth
- Rancid
- Off
- Peachy
- Sour

Using Metaphors and Storytelling – Activity

The most powerful way to develop these skills is to pay attention and listen out for them. Also, observe the impact they have. You should normally see and hear changes in physiology and non-verbal communication (e.g. gestures plus pitch, pace, tonality, emphasis and how they are expressed). You, as the coach, can do this in meetings, chats at work, TV discussions, even plays and films.

A more structured approach is suggested by Zeus and Skiffington (2002). It goes like this:

1. Be alert for, and recognise, the consistent use of the metaphor. For example it is not unusual for a coachee who is feeling under pressure to use language that reflects a battle or war (e.g. worry, losing, being besieged, under attack, being defensive).

2. Point out the use of the metaphor to the coachee.

3. Choose from the following questions to explore the metaphor or story.

(Avoid jumping in with your own version!)

- o what are the implications of the metaphor or story?
- o what impact is this having on the coachee's assumptions, beliefs and feelings?
- o what is the metaphor or story saying about the coachee's current thinking?
- o what is it saying about how the coachee views themselves?
- o what new insights can be gathered by exploring the metaphor or story?
- o how will it improve potential progress?
- o what is the benefit of the metaphor and story to the coachee (and possibly the coach)?
- o can it be further developed to help move things forward?
- o what beliefs and emotions does the metaphor or story reveal?
- o what are the potential limitations within the metaphor or story?
- o what actions does the metaphor suggest?

4. Ask the coachee if they would like to change the metaphor.

5. Work with the coachee to develop a metaphor that is more life-enhancing and beneficial.

6. Ask the coachee to experiment with the new metaphor. Review the results in the next session.

Using Metaphors and Storytelling – Case Study

This involves the use of a well-known metaphor which I use - if appropriate and if the coachee is getting stuck or bogged down in detail.

In this case study, I had a coachee who felt that due to age, plus financial and peer pressure, that they should be changing their career path. They had a number of alternative careers they were considering but became bogged down and couldn't "get their head above the parapet" and were "stuck in a rut", like "running in quicksand". In addition the way they told the story of their life, and career to date, described a situation where they had not made many conscious decisions but had dealt with each situation as it developed with a long term vision or overview.

Rather than pick up on the individual metaphors which I felt would trap us both into too much detail I asked my coachee what would be their ultimate (possibly unrealistic) fantasy. Their response was that they would love to be either invisible or able to fly.

I asked which of these meant more to them and they said flying. I then asked if they had "a good head for heights" and they laughed and said yes.

The next step was to ask them to imagine being a bird, or in a hot air balloon, or a pilot of a helicopter (whichever felt most natural). The coachee then chose to be able to fly like a bird but as themselves.

As we sat in the hotel coffee lounge I asked them to tell me what they could see while they were flying and they proceeded to describe a series of fields and rivers. The next stage was to look down and see themselves walking across the fields and finding ways of getting over the rivers either by bridges, swimming, using a ferry, barge, or jumping. The coachee's change in physiology, voice, and language at this point was dramatic - so I asked them to build a metaphor and story for their future.

Their response was to describe themselves as an explorer, with lots of skills that enabled them to overcome any difficulties they might face. At the same time, they could choose not to go off exploring but stay at home and enjoy being there.

We subsequently used this story as a way forward and the person decided not to change career (but to stay at home) but also to go to night and internet classes and join various voluntary groups to help the elderly and people with learning difficulties.

Using Metaphors and Storytelling – Case Study – Sport

Sport really lends itself to metaphors and storytelling as there are hundreds of gripping and powerful examples that can be used both on an individual and team level. The key is being able to choose effective examples based upon individual and team requirements rather than just rolling out your favourite metaphor and story.

One example saw a coach ask all her players to provide two or three examples of their favourite stories of being in the Zone, not just from their own sports. She then sifted through them to see if any of them cropped up more than once, which inevitably they did. The coach then devoted the first part of the next team meeting to going through the stories and sharing six of them with the squad.

In the second part of the session she broke the squad down into threes and fours and got them to construct a metaphor (e.g. riding the Big Dipper, surfing the wave) and then build these into a future-based short story centred on the season ahead. As an output from this she then had the stories professionally prepared and put into frames and on laminated cards as reminders for the players and support staff.

Since then I have used various versions of this approach in a number of different settings, not just in sport (e.g. with sales teams, at conferences, with accountants!).

Using Metaphors and Storytelling – Sample Dialogue

Coach: So, what would you say is your ultimate fantasy?

Coachee: (laughs) Do you mean sexual?

Coach: (laughs) Possibly. What's interesting is how few ultimate fantasies are actually sexual. Tell me about yours – in whatever realm.

Coachee: I guess - like a lot of people - I would like to be able to fly or be invisible. That would be the ultimate Zone experience.

Coach: Which of the two is the biggest one?

Coachee: Flying, I guess.

Coach: Have you a good head for heights? (laughs)

Coachee: (laughs) Oh yes, I could deal with being a high flyer.

Coach: How does it relate to your experiences of being in the Zone?

Coachee: Well, when I am in the Zone it is like being able to fly.

Coach: Because you are on automatic pilot? (laughs)

Coachee: (grins) Nice one, but yes it is actually.

Coach: So should we play around with this and see how we can use it to help you get into the Zone more regularly?

Coachee: Yes, that would be great.

Coach: The first thing I would suggest is that we freewheel around it for a bit and then try and pin it down to something more specific and tangible. How does that sound?

Coachee: Great, let's go for it.

Coach: Okay, firstly I'd like you to see yourself as a bird, or in a hot air balloon, or even as a helicopter pilot. Whichever works best for you.

Coachee: Let's go for the bird thing but with me actually doing the flying – like Superman, that would be perfect.

Coach: Okay, let's start…

Developing Your Own Coaching Style

A constant theme of this book has been the importance of being aware of theory and models but above all being practical, coachee-oriented, and not slavish to one way of doing things or one answer. To most coaches this sounds obvious yet it is very easy for even the best coaches to fall into this trap.

Oddly the best way to avoid being 'one size fits all' or prescriptive is to pay absolute attention to the coachee and their needs and requirements. This really helps in removing the complications of any blockages the coach may create, however inadvertently. Some coaches would argue that this whole topic is misplaced, that the coach should not have an obvious style; they should be a cipher merely responding to the needs of the coachee and the situations.

To me this is unrealistic; everybody has their own personality and way of doing things. In order to be effective the coach should be true to these, but not at the expense of their purpose. They should maximise their strengths but be aware of their weaknesses. For example, many coaches enjoy talking and, when carried out appropriately, that's fine. But when overdone, even if it's based on good intentions, it will prove counterproductive.

The most effective style is likely to be based upon the points covered in this book, in particular using the key interpersonal skills in an appropriate and effective way. A very good summary regarding the importance of having your own style of coaching is in the Jerry Lynch book *Creative Coaching* (2001) which although based on sport is true for other contexts as well. *"Creative coaches are passionate, selfless, and focused on the good of those they coach. Different coaching styles can accommodate these character traits – you do not need to change the style that works for you. Instead, simply look for ways to instil these into your existing repertoire."*

Developing Your Own Coaching Style – Activity

1. Review your current coaching style and be aware of its key strengths and weaknesses.
2. Review the interpersonal skills in this book and plan to further develop the ones that are important to you.
3. Work even harder on paying attention to your coachee and responding accordingly. See what impact this has on your thinking and style.
4. Watch how other people use and respond to your style.

Developing Your Own Coaching Style – Case Study

The coachee in this situation was MD of a division within a multi-national company. He was used to getting his own way and being listened to, which he then construed as agreement to what he had said and a commitment to action.

In our first two sessions things felt uneasy to me and I felt I was not drawing him out, or establishing his true needs. At the third session he asked me what I thought of him. By the manner in which he said this, it was obvious he expected me to be wishy washy and vague in my reply. I told him that his style alienated a lot of people including me at this point and that - based upon observing him with his people - I didn't think other people really understood what he wanted.

He reacted forcefully to this and said it was nonsense and people understood him perfectly. My next question, therefore, asked him: "Did people always do exactly what he wanted and expected?". His response was: "Of course not", but if he kept telling them in the end they got it, although this took time and energy.

We left it there and agreed to review his style next time. Normally we didn't have much contact between sessions so this time I sent him three or four articles on the style of his heroes – Steve Jobs, Richard Branson, John Timpson, and asked him to comment. I also asked him to do a 360° profile and get six of his colleagues to complete the 360° on him (with guaranteed anonymity). When he got the feedback, which confirmed our discussion points, he disagreed forcefully and would not accept it.

Instead of browbeating him or giving way I asked him review why he had volunteered for the coaching, whether he wanted to continue, and how he would feel if he stopped. In other words I treated 'fire with fire' but with depth, evidence, and a future orientation. He agreed to stay in the coaching and to give it a go. The coaching continues to this day.

Developing Your Own Coaching Style – Case Study – Sport

It's not unusual in any context that when someone gets promoted they imitate and copy, possibly without meaning to, either the person they have taken over from or some other role model they have had experience of. There is nothing necessarily wrong with this - however, at some point in time, it will become necessary to become your own person and have your own coaching style.

This is as true in sport as in any other situation; in fact possibly more so due to the public visibility of many managerial and coaching roles and the way the public view them. Many managers and coaches will admit to having got it wrong in their early days in the job. Some would even go so far as to admit they didn't really have a style of their own at the beginning of their careers.

Whenever I consider this topic I am reminded of the coach whose hero had been Sir Alex Ferguson. In his first twelve to eighteen months in the job, whenever he came up against a problem, he thought 'what would Sir Alex Ferguson do in this situation?' In many ways this is totally understandable; the issue was, of course, he didn't know the answer. At best it was a guess.

As time went by, partially through bitter experience, he developed his own way of doing things and, while not always getting things absolutely right, he did at least know he had made his own choices.

The key to matters was his interest in the Zone. He had experienced the Zone many times as a player and knew enough about it to realise that, although some of the processes involved for getting into the Zone are broadly applicable, at the end of the day everybody finds their own way of achieving it. This gave him the confidence to apply this to his management and coaching style as well.

The Impact of Your Own Behaviour in Coaching For The Zone

Quote: A lot of people mistake a short memory for a clear conscience Unknown

One of the debates that surrounds coaching, and this can apply particularly to the Zone, is whether the coach needs to be an expert in the field they are coaching (i.e. if you are coaching an accountant do you need to be an accountant yourself in order to be effective?)

One way of looking at this question is to consider whether people who are excellent in their chosen field are equipped to help others learn that skill. In other words, does being good at something necessarily mean that you are able to coach it?

Sport offers some interesting examples of this. Most of the Premier League's soccer managers have been professional footballers but most of them did not have particularly distinguished careers, yet they have developed the skills to coach others to achieve higher levels than they themselves did.

Some people would go further and argue that knowing a lot, particularly technically, about a role can actually inhibit the effectiveness of the coach as there is a danger that they will be restricted by their own knowledge and/or impose their own experiences on the coachee (rather than help them develop their own).

With regard to the Zone this is even more important. Of course it can be helpful for the coach to have experienced the Zone and to understand how they achieved it. However, as the Zone can be a highly individual, subjective, hard-to-define experience, the coach runs the same risk as the accountant coaching the accountant: their own skills and knowledge actually get in the way of their effectiveness.

The impact of any coach's behaviour, particularly regarding the Zone, is in their use and application of the skills covered in this section of the book. Drawing out the experiences of the coachee helps them make more explicit (to develop and understand) the processes that allow them to be repeated.

There is a difference between being aware of the impact of your own behaviour and being a role model, although of course they can coincide. If the coach sets out to be 'perfect' it's likely that this will get in the way of the coachee achieving the Zone because it will be more about the coach than the coachee. Ironically the best chance the coach has of helping the coachee get into the Zone is to do what comes naturally and rely on their skills and judgement.

The key behaviours that the coach needs to demonstrate when they work with the coachee include:

- Being supportive
- Demonstrating openness
- Showing belief in the coachee
- Being trusting
- Being authentic
- Learning from failure(s)
- Demonstrating respect – for both the coachee and the process
- Being flexible
- Showing tenacity
- Focussing on solutions
- Being proactive
- Putting the coachee first
- Being self-aware
- Creating empathy
- Being resourceful

The Impact of Your Own Behaviour in Coaching For The Zone – Case Study – Sport

This example follows on from the one used in the previous section – Developing Your Own Coaching Style. In that case study the new coach had used Sir Alex Ferguson as a role model and wondered what he would do in any given situation. Finally by using his experience of the Zone he was able to find his own way of doing things.

A crucial part of this was him becoming increasingly aware of the impact of his own behaviour on other people. His experiences of the Zone had helped him realise that, in the end, people find their own way of achieving it, something he forgot in his early days in the job. Consequently he had a number of disputes with players who didn't want to do things his way regarding the Zone, finally realising he was doing to them what he hadn't liked when it had been done to him.

Although he was shocked and disappointed with himself for doing this, he was open with the players regarding his intent for doing things this way, told them he realised he hadn't been getting it right, and agreed with them how best to move things forward. This became a key element in his recognition of the impact of his own behaviour.

The Impact of Your Own Behaviour in Coaching For The Zone – Activity

This is an NLP activity called the New Behaviour Generator which can be used both personally and with a coachee. As part of helping people get into the Zone, the breakthrough point may well be helping them develop new, more resourceful behaviours.

1. Chose the specific behaviour you want to change, develop, or have for the first time.

2. Ask "how would I/you look, sound and feel if I/you were carrying out this behaviour effectively?" Imagine yourself doing it in the specific situation you want. Live the whole experience across all your senses. If for some reason you cannot see, hear or feel yourself doing the behaviour, imagine someone you know who is good at it, or even, someone from a TV programme or film; the key point is that any form of representation will

help and assist the process.

3. If there is something that is not quite right, keep running it through your mind making any necessary changes and keep doing this until it is working for you. You are performing as you want to be.

4. When the imagined performance is working for you, go inside the experience (i.e. become associated).

5. As you run it through in an associated state be in touch with all your senses.

6. If for any reason you need to modify anything, step out (i.e. become disassociated), make the necessary adjustments, then step back in (i.e. become associated and check it out).

7. Ask yourself: "How will I know by seeing, hearing and feeling that it is the right time to use the new behaviour?" – decide on the signal(s).

8. Imagine that the signal has taken place, you have used your new behaviour. It has worked. Be aware of how you feel.

The Impact of Your Own Behaviour in Coaching For The Zone – Case Study

The situation in this case study was a little unusual in that I was coaching a friend who was also a client. Normally in Executive Coaching you do not know the coachee at the beginning of the process.

In this case it was a friend who joined a company that used me as an executive coach and without really thinking about it I took for granted certain things about his personality (e.g. his willingness to try new things, his self-awareness, his honesty). What I forgot about was the context! It was work not pleasure, and more importantly it was a new job where he was desperate to impress.

The consequences of this were that my behaviour was the same as in our social interactions (i.e. light-hearted and fairly unstructured). This resulted in intense frustration on his part, frustration on my part because 'he didn't seem to be getting it' and no real progress.

Key Skills

This was only changed and improved when the penny dropped for me and I asked him how he felt it was going and how we could improve things.

One of the outputs from this conversation was that he told me I often referred to the Zone but at no time had I explained it or gone into how to achieve it. Once we had established he had experienced the Zone in his sports and hobbies, we were able to work towards it in his work situation.

The Impact of Your Own Behaviour in Coaching For The Zone – Sample Dialogue

Coach: How do you feel, so far, about how the coaching is going?

Coachee: (hesitates) To be honest it's not what I expected.

Coach: Oh, why is that?

Coachee: It's more like going out for a pint and having a cosy chat. Is that how it's supposed to be?

Coach: Sometimes it can be a bit like that but not normally. The important thing is making it work for you.

Coachee: Okay, well I would like more structure, and a clearer agenda for each session.

Coach: Anything else?

Coachee: Well as we are talking about it, you often mention the Zone and I know the coaching is partly about that. But I don't really understand it and you haven't really explained it to me.

Coach: Fair point [explains Zone]. Do you think this is relevant to you and your situation?

Coachee: Absolutely, I've experienced it outside work so I would be interested in seeing how I can use it at work.

Coach: Excellent, so let's start by looking at situations where being in the Zone would be helpful.

Reviewing and Learning from Coaching for the Zone

There are a number of aspects to this. Normally there is more than enough for both the coach and coachee to learn from the coaching itself, so adding in the lessons learnt regarding the Zone can significantly add to the amount of learning involved.

Reviewing and learning are the cornerstones of effective ongoing development and without them, any coaching, whether it be for the Zone or not, will not impact as much as it could do. This is complicated by the fact that people lead increasingly busy lives which can leave little time for reflection. Therefore it is even more important that reviewing and learning are included in the coaching process.

As with all other aspects of the coaching process it is helpful if the coach has knowledge of the appropriate frameworks and models without being slavish to any of them, so that everything can be fine-tuned to the coachee.

With regard to learning there are a number of models available. Dr Peter Honey's aforementioned Learning Styles Inventory is one of them. This provides feedback on whether the coachee has a preference for either Activist, Pragmatist, Theorist or Reflector ways of learning.

Reviewing can be a natural process, however just hoping that it will happen is too haphazard to be of any real benefit. In order to give the process some structure I would recommend that the coachee (and the coach) allocate say 10 minutes per day to reviewing the day's events: what was planned, what actually happened, etc. This should include writing some brief notes that capture the main points pinning down what was actually learnt and how it could be applied in the future. This is particularly important when working with the Zone as it allows time to 'unpick' key lessons from the process.

Reviewing and Learning from Coaching for the Zone – Case Study

The coachee in this example was a successful manager working for a Housing Association. She played a lot of sport outside work and was a highly regarded badminton coach.

She was fascinated by the potential overlap of being able to achieve the Zone at work as well as in her sport (while coaching). At the start of the coaching process she made it very clear that this was an expectation she had and was hungry to get started. Something in her eagerness made me think that she might want to charge into anything we did and that the key to sustained success might be to get her to slow down and review more.

Therefore I decided to use the Learning Styles Inventory referred to earlier and see what she thought of it. Her initial reaction was mild interest, but she was convinced that learning 'just happened' and planning to do it might actually inhibit the chances of it occurring.

The results of the LSI suggested she was very high on being an Activist and Pragmatist and very low on Reflector and Theorist. She saw this as confirmation that the LSI was pretty accurate but what difference did it make?

I shared my view that while it was more than possible to get into the Zone from an Activist or Pragmatist position, I had the hunch that, in her case, developing the Theorist and Reflector positions might be the key. Based on this she agreed to do 10 minute-a-day review sessions and, in particular, on Theorist and Reflector aspects. Specifically we agreed that this would be done on the Zone work as part of a wider review of what was working.

Initially she struggled with doing this, not with planning the time (easy for an Activist/Pragmatist) but in keeping her mind focused on the more subjective aspects of her experiences. Over a period of a few weeks this became a habitual, natural part of her day and the Pragmatist in her started to see the benefits. She then started to extend this process into the rest of her work and subsequently achieved her goal of being able to get into the Zone in a number of work-based situations.

Reviewing and Learning from Coaching for the Zone – Activity

1. Learn about two or three learning models and test them on yourself.
2. Where appropriate use them with your coachees.
3. Develop the habit of keeping your own Learning Log and use this to improve your coaching for the Zone.
4. Reflect and write up your own experiences of the Zone.
5. Plan to get into the Zone in situations where it hasn't happened before.
6. Buy one or two books on the Zone and write up your observations. Also do this after watching people being interviewed on TV about achieving the Zone or higher than normal levels of performance.

Reviewing and Learning from Coaching for the Zone – Sample Dialogue

Coachee: I feel comfortable that the LSI is accurate for me but how does that impact on me getting into the Zone?

Coach: That's a really good question. In my experience it's more than possible to get into the Zone from an Activist/Pragmatist style, however, and this is just my experience I've never researched this, the people who get into the Zone on a more regular, consistent basis often seem to be able to do it because they are high on Reflector, or work on using and developing the Reflector style.

Coachee: So it may not be natural to them but they can still use it to help get into the Zone.

Coach: That's right. Some people can access the Zone without using the Reflector style but most seem to need it.

Coachee: So what should I do?

Coach: What do you think?

Coachee: I guess I need to plan in some 'formal time' for reflection.

Coach: You don't sound very excited by the prospect of doing that.

Coachee: I'm not but that is my way of working. So, if I plan to do it I will. Can I start by doing it just on the Zone work - to start off with - then see how it goes?

Coach: Absolutely. Let's decide how and when you will do it.

Measuring and Evaluating Coaching for the Zone

There are many ways of measuring and evaluating the success of coaching. Normally this would breakdown into two areas: quantitative and qualitative.

In many organisations there is a strong emphasis on the quantitative. The obvious reason for this is that it tends to be easier and can therefore be used to justify the money spent on it. This is fine and perfectly understandable but may not paint the whole picture.

Most ways of quantitative measurement break down into a combination of hard edged factors e.g. a reduction in customer complaints, increases in performance, profits, etc. In addition, other relevant factors such as cost and time are often used as well.

However some aspects of this, particularly when measuring the Zone, can create difficulties. If a coacheee is working on confidence, or making a better/quicker impact on people, or feeling more comfortable in a meeting with senior managers, these can be difficult to measure in a quantitative way.

To the coachee it often doesn't matter that there aren't any hard measures, they are comfortable that they will know the difference. This is entirely valid for the individual but can make the success of the coaching difficult to prove. For example a centre forward in football might feel better about his all-round game and contribution but, if they aren't scoring many goals, it may not matter as they are paid for scoring goals.

Many books on coaching don't even mention measurement or evaluation but this is ducking the issue. Rather, I believe that being open about the difficulties of the issue, but standing firm that if someone believes their confidence has moved from 4/10 to 7/10 – is sufficient. As a consequence of this it may then be possible to move onto tackling an issue or situation which is more obviously measurable (e.g., by using 360° feedback).

Where measurement and evaluation are possible they are normally carried for a combination of the following reasons:

- To demonstrate performance improvement for an individual, department, or organisation as a result of coaching
- To demonstrate the cost-effectiveness of coaching compared with other forms of development (such as training)
- To enable the coach to demonstrate their effectiveness

Some of the areas that are often measured and evaluated include:

- Costs – these can include the coach, coach's time, administration, design, materials
- Changes to the coachee's performance or behaviour or performance. These can include career progression, skills and knowledge acquisition, retaining more people, more effective recruitment, handling stress and pressure better, managing personal energy more effectively, building a team, managing change, work/life balance, creativity, and health.

Some of the classic ways to measure and evaluate outcomes include:

- The organisation's performance management (appraisal) process
- 360° feedback
- Line Manager reports
- Specific projects
- Interviews
- The coachee's own opinions
- Observation
- Return on Investment
- Cost Benefit Analysis

I have deliberately dwelt on the usual ways of measuring and evaluating coaching and a lot of these can apply to the Zone. However the Zone creates a range of other issues, the main one being how to measure subjective experience. It is obviously quite possible to have a measurable outcome from being in the Zone (e.g. the centre forward scoring more goals, the team winning more games, improved costs and efficiencies). Sometimes, though, the successful outcomes from being in the Zone may not be as demonstrably measurable (e.g. feeling better or more empowered about oneself).

Being clear at the beginning of the coaching with the coachee, the manager, the HR manager, the organisation, plus relevant others, is therefore a key step. Many people are already aware of this, particularly with the Zone, and happy to use their own judgement and observations to decide to what extent the coaching is impacting.

With the Zone my normal style is to measure and evaluate as objectively as possible, but also to encourage the more subjective qualitative aspects. For example in the case mentioned earlier - if the coachee believed they had moved their confidence from 4/10 to 7/10, I would push them hard to be as concrete as possible about the evidence for this and to translate their experiences into something that was demonstrable.

Measuring and Evaluating Coaching for the Zone – Case Study

This case study revolved around a medium-sized marketing agency which had built its success around creative ideas and fantastic levels of customer service. This had taken the agency to employing about 25 people at which point the MD felt he was struggling to know and manage everyone as well as he had previously. He also felt the same about the number and type of their clients. In consequence he began paying a lot more attention to his clients but his people, for the first time, were not able to translate his thoughts and ideas into what the clients really wanted.

I had started to coach him as a consequence of a referral from a friend of his, who he played golf with and had been on skiing holidays with. His friend had used the coaching to work on the Zone both in his business and sporting lives and this balance appealed to the agency MD.

In discussing the situation in his company the MD felt that the 'pizzazz' was going out of it and wondered if this was due to the increased numbers involved. My response was that I worked in organisations of many thousands where the 'pizzazz' was still there, so numbers might be a factor but they didn't explain the whole situation.

After this discussion he decided to set up a Think Tank of half a dozen people from across the company and that I should run a workshop on pizzazz (which became our term for the Zone). At the workshop we did a modified version of the long established Boston Matrix and combined this with a Culture Style Profile, with the promise that the results of this would be fed back to all employees so that everyone could contribute and feel engaged.

In addition each attendee at the workshop was appointed as a Pizzazz Champion to spread the word regarding our progress (remember this was a Marketing Agency!).

At the end of the workshop the topic of measurement and evaluation was discussed with a range of opinions expressed, ranging from: "It doesn't matter because we will know" to "If we don't measure and evaluate we will be copping out". This split of opinion was evident throughout the company and while not a major issue had the potential to become one of those niggling points that can slow down or impede the changes required.

One of the Pizzazz Champions was tasked to investigate the options and came up with a combination of traditional approaches (i.e. interviews, randomly chosen 360° feedback from clients). The key ingredient was the 'Pizzazz Scale' that he developed based upon seven factors with measures for each one. The scale covered topics such as: fun, creativity, impact, challenge and accurately reflected what the business stood for.

In addition the MD implemented a 'Delegation for Pizzazz' initiative where he attempted to delegate more and receive regular feedback on how effective he was being.

The outcome from the overall process was that the business got back to a version of its core values (modified and updated) which it was able to demonstrate and share with its clients.

One lesson for me, as someone who works with the Zone on a regular basis, was to accept 'Pizzazz' as being meaningful and relevant (i.e. that the word doesn't matter but the effect and impact does).

Measuring and Evaluating the Success of Coaching for the Zone – Case Study – Sport

In the main body of this section we have mentioned a number of approaches to dealing with this topic and all of them can be relevant (dependent on the context or situation).

This case study is about a golfer I worked with who was a particularly analytical character and was very concerned about how best to measure the impact of being in the Zone more regularly, and see what it had achieved for him. He was comfortable with the subjective parts of knowing he had been in the Zone and how that had impacted on his results but wanted more data on what it had done to the content of his game.

One of the great things about golf, as well as many other sports, is the amount of data, including video analysis that is available. One of the things we did was to spend a day going through the data on his performances before and after he started working on the Zone.

We developed a number of measures for this. Ones which he felt would tell him what he was getting right (and wrong) as well as the actual finishing place/money earned, which were the ones he traditionally had used.

Among the measures were, the length of his drives, the number of putts taken, the distance he was putting from, the number of times he hit the fairway, his scores per round over the four rounds of a competition, etc. All of these were available to him previously, but he hadn't really used them and certainly hadn't used them in the context of measuring and evaluating the Zone.

Measuring and Evaluating the Success of Coaching for the Zone – Activity

Based upon the case study one of the lessons is to match the approach of measurement and evaluation to the individual, department or organisation. At the same time you need to be willing to challenge them to be different, go further if the situation requires it, and push them to not take the easy option.

Next Steps: Integrating the Zone into your Coaching

Try – Fail – Try Again – Fail better

Samuel Beckett

Overview

The purpose of this book has been to help you assist your coachees (and yourself) to get into the Zone more frequently and consistently.

In order for that to become a natural, habitual, process it is worth revisiting a few key points:

- The Zone is difficult to describe
- There is a chance that if you realise, at any given moment, that you are in the Zone, you may well come out of it
- Although the Zone has some common elements (e.g. a sense of timelessness, ease in performance, a feeling of going beyond oneself) it is still a highly individualised experience
- There is no one 'right' way to get into the Zone; each person can find their own best way
- You may not be able to get your coachees into the Zone on every occasion, *but* you will be able to help them achieve it more frequently and consistently
- Your beliefs regarding the Zone will be a key factor in helping you achieve this

- Your skillset will be a major factor *but* it is the application of these skills that will be key (i.e. being skilled in listening, or asking good quality questions, is extremely helpful but listening for listening's sake or asking a really good question *at the wrong time* will only damage your ability to help your coachee get into the Zone).
- Having an open mind to trying new ways of achieving your goals, as a coach, will help you move forward.

The Importance of Preparation

A constant theme of this book has been the importance of being as prepared as possible. Many people have had the experience of delivering a presentation, carrying out an appraisal, getting ready for a big game, preparing for a holiday and then, at the most important moment, realising they were not as prepared as they should be.

The common explanation for this is 'there just wasn't enough time to prepare properly' but without preparation - performance will suffer and relationships and credibility will be damaged. One of the difficulties regarding preparation is that it is often 'invisible', (i.e. no one knows we are doing it). This may be true but unfortunately *everyone* will know if we haven't done it properly.

Preparation can be easier in the sporting world because more time is allocated to it. However, often that time is used for physical/technical aspects of the game at the expense of mental preparation.

One example of giving all aspects of preparation their right emphasis is the 2014 Golf Ryder Cup between Europe and the USA. Both before, during and after the competition the European Players emphasised how well their Captain, Paul McGinley had prepared, right down to the quotes around the walls of the team room. I have not heard or read any specific comments that individual players and/or the team were in the Zone but it would be hard to believe that at some important moments they were not.

Developing A Structured Approach To Coaching People Get Into The Zone

For each coach this may mean different things, and each coach will need to focus on different parts of this book in order to find their own 'best way.' In fact, you may need to continually change and modify the coaching path dependent on the requirements of your coachee.

Success will likely stem from your ability to:

- Read the situation your coachee wants to deal with
- Read your coachee's skills, attitudes, beliefs, blockages, goals
- Be self-aware enough to be flexible in how you help them move forward
- Be self-aware enough to know your own limitations
- Prove willing to push yourself into new territory in order to help your coachee

An Outline Framework For Coaching People To Get Into The Zone

One of the reasons this book is structured in the way it, is so a coach can develop a framework in order to help them check and/or improve their skills in getting people into the Zone. The Sessions, Activities, Case Studies, and Sample Dialogues should help facilitate this.

There are three important points to make regarding how best to use the Sessions and Key Skills covered in this book:

1. The checklists and activities used in Sessions 1-8 are in an order that should best help a coachee get into the Zone. Therefore it is suggested that, unless deemed unnecessary, they should be followed sequentially.

An example of this is the checklist covered in Session One which is shown below.

Before meeting the coachee for the first time carry out a personal audit of your own experiences and history both as a coach and with regard to being in/helping others achieve the Zone

- What key skills do I want to work on in order to become a better coach e.g. creating rapport, questioning, influencing, etc?
- In the past, what skills have worked for me?
- What are my own experiences of being in the Zone? What impact did this have on me and my performance ?
- What else do I need to know about the Zone?
- What specific part of coaching for the Zone do I want to work on in order to improve my own effectiveness?
- Who else do I need to involve?
- What setbacks have I previously overcome and how can I use them to help me next time?
- What did I learn about myself that I didn't know already?
- What can I do to improve my levels of success next time?
- How will I measure the improved level of success next time?
- What do I want to work on (if anything) that I haven't previously tried?
- What can I do to ensure that coaching for the Zone is a fun and productive process?
- How will I reward myself for my success?
- How can I plan my time to ensure that I use it purposefully?
- What relaxation techniques will I use to keep me fresh and focussed?

This example is repeated so that the coach can see the importance of having a framework in place without being trapped by it. So the criteria for using the checklists covered in the Sessions are:

a) They add value to the process
b) They provide the coach with ideas or information they wouldn't normally have had
c) They enable the coach to help the coachee achieve the coachee's goals

2. The specific skills covered in the Sessions e.g. anchoring, visualisation, affirmations, etc, may not be required at all (although this is unlikely) but may be required outside the order of the Sessions covered in this book.

It will be the skill of the coach in reading what is required that will determine this.

3. The same will apply to the Key Skills sections of this book. All of the Key Skills could apply, some may apply some of the time and there may be times when it feels as though none of them apply (but they will)!

As you would expect, the key to all of this is the skill and judgement of the coach. The coach who is prepared, has the relevant skills, is willing to explore new challenges, has positive beliefs regarding their own skills and the (sometimes latent) abilities of their coachees is in an outstanding position to impact on those they deal with.

Remember that the Zone is a transformative experience. One that changes people, improves the quality of their experiences, and frees them up to go beyond anything they thought they might ever achieve. The role of the coach in helping them achieve this is a vital and fulfilling one that also allows the coach to improve the quality of their own experiences and skills.

Bibliography and Suggested Reading

Abrahams, D. (2012), *Soccer Tough: Simple Football Psychology to Improve Your Game*, Birmingham: Bennion Kearny

Beauregard, M. (2012), *Brain Wars: The Scientific Battle Over the Existence of the Mind and the Proof That Will Change the Way We Live Our Lives*, New York: Harper One

Bull, S, J., Albinson, J. G., and Shambrook, C.J. (1996), *The Mental Game Plan: Getting Psyched For Sport*, Cheltenham: Sports Dynamics

Butler, R. J. (1996), *Sports Psychology in Action*, Oxford: Butterworth–Heinemann

Cialdini, R. B. (1988), *Influence – Science and Practice*, London: Harper Collins

Cooper, A. (1998), *Playing in the Zone: Exploring the Spiritual Dimensions of Sport*, Boston: Shambhala Publications

Corey, G. (2002), *The Skilled Helper*, Pacific Grove: Brooks/Cole

Csikszentmihalyi, M. (1993), *The Evolving Self*, New York: Hardy Perennial

Csikszentmihalyi, M. (1990), *Flow: The Psychology of Optimal Experience*, New York: Harper and Row

De Rond, M. (2012), *There Is An I In Team: What Elite Athletes & Coaches Really Know About High Performance*, Boston MA, Harvard Business Review Press

Downey, M. (1999), *Effective Coaching*, London: Open Business Books

Dweck, C. (2006), *Mindset: How You Can Fulfil Your Potential*, New York: Ballantine

Bibliography

Ellis, A., and Dryden, W. (1999), *The Practice of Rational Emotive Behaviour Therapy*, London: Free Association Books.

Flaherty, J. (1999), *Coaching – Evoking Excellence in Others*, Woburn MA: Butterworth–Heinemann

Garratt, T. (1999), *Sporting Excellence: Optimising Sports Performance Using NLP*, Carmarthen Wales: Crown House Publishing

Gilson, C., Pratt, M., Roberts, K., and Weymes, E, (2000), *Peak Performance: Business Lessons From The World's Top Sports Organisations*, London: Harper Collins

Goldberg, A. S. (1998), *Sports Slump Busting*, Champaign IL: Human Kinetics

Hall, L. (2013), *Mindful Coaching: How Mindfulness Can Transform Coaching Practice*, London: Kogan Page

Hardy, L., Jones, G., and Gould, D. (1996), *Understanding Psychological Preparation for Sport: Theory and Practice of Elite Performers*, Chichester: Wiley

Hay, J. (1999), *Transformational Mentoring*, Watford: Sherwood Publishing

Honey, P., and Mumford, A. (2001), *Learning Styles Questionnaire*, Maidenhead: Peter Honey Publications

Ibarra, H. (2004), *Working Identity: Unconventional Strategies for Reinventing Your Career*, Boston MA: Harvard Business Press

Kahneman, D. (2011), *Thinking Fast and Slow*, London: Penguin Books

Kilburg, R.R. (2002), *Executive Coaching : Developing Managerial Wisdom in a World of Chaos*, Washington DC: American Psychological Association

Kinlaw, D. (1990), *Coaching for Commitment*, San Diego: University Associates

Kline, N. (1999), *Time to Think*, London: Cassell Illustrated

Koole, W. (2014), *Mindful Leadership: Effective Tools to Help You Focus & Succeed*, Amsterdam: Warden Press

Lynch, J. (2001), *Creative Coaching*, Champaign IL: Human Kinetics

Loder, S. J., and Snyder, C.R. (2003), *Positive Psychological Assessment: A Handbook of Models and Measures*, Washington DC: American Psychological Association

Maslow, A. H., (1987), *Motivation & Personality*, 3rd edition., New York: Harper & Row

McDermott, I., and Jago, W. (2001), *The NLP Coach*, London: Piatkus

Mruk, C. (1999), *Self Esteem: Research, Theory and Practice*, London: Free Association Books

Mulry, R. (1995), *In The Zone*, Arlington Virginia: Great Ocean Publishers

Nideffer, R. M. (2001), *Getting into the Optimal Performance State*, San Diego CA: Enhanced Performance Systems

Orlick, T. (2000), *In Pursuit of Excellence*, Champaign IL: Human Kinetics

Peters, S. (2012), *The Chimp Paradox*, London, Ebury Publishing

Petier, B. (2001), *The Psychology of Executive Coaching*, New York: Brunner – Routledge

Rogers, C. (1983), *Freedom to Learn*, Columbus,: Charles E Merrill

Rowan, J. (1993), *The Transpersonal – Psychotherapy and Counselling*, London: Brunner – Routledge

Statt, D.A. (2000), *Using Psychology in Management Training*, London: Routledge

Stevens, R. (Ed) (1996), *Understanding the Self*, London: Sage Publications

Stewart, I. (2000), *Transactional Analysis*, Counselling in Action, London: Sage Publications

Turner, M,. Barker, J, (2014), *What Business Can Learn From Sport Psychology*, Oakamoor, Bennion Kearny

Bibliography

Van Schalkwyk, J. (2004), *On Track to the Top*, North Ryde NSW: McGraw Hill

Vernachia, R., McGuire, R., and Cook, D. (1996), *Coaching Mental Excellence*, Portola Valley CA: Warde Publishers

Whitmore, J. (1996), *Coaching for Performance*, London: Nicholas Brearley

Wilson, R.A. (2002), *Quantum Psychology: How Brian Software Programs You & Your World*, Temple, Arizona: New Falcon Publications

Williams, M., Penman, D, (2011), *Mindfulness: A Practical Guide to Finding Peace in a Frantic World*, London: Piatkus

Williams, N. (1999), *The Work We Were Born To Do*, London: Element Books

Woodward, C. (2004), *Winning*, London: Hodder & Stoughton

Zeus, P., and Skiffington, S., (2002), *Coaching at Work Toolkit*, Roseville NSW: McGraw Hill

Soccer Tough by Dan Abrahams

"Take a minute to slip into the mind of one of the world's greatest soccer players and imagine a stadium around you. Picture a performance under the lights and mentally play the perfect game."

Technique, speed and tactical execution are crucial components of winning soccer, but it is mental toughness that marks out the very best players – the ability to play when pressure is highest, the opposition is strongest, and fear is greatest. Top players and coaches understand the importance of sport psychology in soccer but how do you actually train your mind to become the best player you can be? Soccer Tough demystifies this crucial side of the game and offers practical techniques that will enable soccer players of all abilities to actively develop focus, energy, and confidence. Soccer Tough will help banish the fear, mistakes, and mental limits that holds players back.

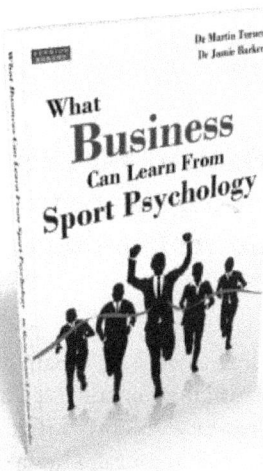

★ ★ ★ ★ ★ ▾ (57)

(Amazon.co.uk Oct 2014)

What Business Can Learn From Sport Psychology
by Dr Martin Turner & Dr Jamie Barker

The mental side of performance has always been a crucial component for success – but nowadays coaches, teams, and athletes of all levels and abilities are using sport psychology to help fulfil their potential and serve up success.

In What Business Can Learn From Sport Psychology readers will develop the most important weapon needed to succeed in business: their mental approach to performance. This book reveals the secrets of the winning mind by exploring the strategies and techniques used by the most successful athletes and professionals on the planet. Based on decades of scientific research, the authors' professional experiences, and the experiences of winning athletes and business professionals, this book is a practical and evidence-driven resource that will teach readers how to deal with pressure, break through adversity, embrace challenges, project business confidence, and much more..

★ ★ ★ ★ ★ ▾ (6)

(Amazon.co.uk Oct 2014)

Other Bennion Kearny Books

The 7 Master Moves of Success
by Jag Shoker

In this absorbing and uplifting book, Jag Shoker – a leading performance coach to business leaders, sports professionals and creative performers – brings the science and inspiration behind success to life. He reveals the 7 Master Moves that combine to create the high performance state that he calls Inspired Movement: the ability to perform an optimal series of moves to create the success you desire most. Drawing widely on scientific research, his extensive consultancy experiences, and insights into the successes of top performers in business, sport, and entertainment, 7 Master Moves is a synthesis of the leading-edge thinking, and paradigms, that underpin personal performance and potential. Building upon key research in fields such as neuroscience, psychology, expert performance and talent development - 7 Master Moves represents an evidence-based 'meta' theory of what really works. Compelling to read, and easy to follow, the book incorporates a strong practical element and shares a number of powerful and practical exercises that can help you apply each Master Move and achieve greater results in your life and work.

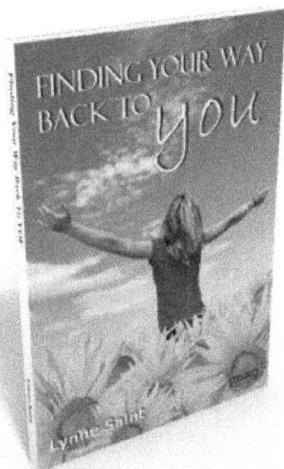

★ ★ ★ ★ ★ ▾ (8)

(Amazon.co.uk Oct 2014)

Finding Your Way Back to YOU: A self-help book for women who want to regain their Mojo and realise their dreams! by Lynne Saint

Designed as a practical book with an accompanying downloadable journal and weblinked exercises, Finding Your Way Back to YOU introduces Neuro-Linguistic Programming, and Cognitive Behavioural Therapy techniques for women's change. It will help readers to develop and achieve the goals they dreamed of and show them how to increase self-confidence - removing any self-limiting beliefs that previously prevented them from getting what they want. The author is an experienced life coach, NLP Practitioner and Hypnotherapist.

★ ★ ★ ★ ★ ▾ (4)

(Amazon.co.uk Oct 2014)

www.ingramcontent.com/pod-product-compliance
Lightning Source LLC
Chambersburg PA
CBHW062042090426
42740CB00016B/2994